Endorsements

I love everything about *The Happy Prophet*, even down to the title and the font. Keith begins this book with Luke 9:54, one of the best examples we have of Jesus correcting His disciples. The disciples wanted to bring death as punishment, but Jesus rebuked them, saying, "We are here to save lives, not destroy lives."

Heaven is full of joy. The Bible says that Jesus endured the cross for the joy set before Him. We, as His children, should hold onto joy and apply it to everything in our lives. I believe this book will help many to see with new eyes—eyes that give life and joy to those around them. Good job, Keith!

—Beni Johnson
Bethel Church, Redding, CA
Author of *The Happy Intercessor, Healthy and Free,* and *40 Days To Wholeness*

The Happy Prophet is an exciting reminder of God's joyful design for New Covenant prophets. Keith removes performance-based mindsets as he points to the incredible view offered from the right side of the Cross where we, who have been co-seated in heavenly places, can remain filled with a trusting faith that comes from our loving Father.

The pages in this book are filled with wisdom and insights that will help you live a prophetic lifestyle in an honest, authentic way, and to sustain your joy in every circumstance. You will be encouraged and inspired.

Let the Happy Prophets arise!

—Georgian Banov
Valrico, FL
President, and Co-Founder of Global Celebration

What a great book! Keith Ferrante keeps upgrading our understanding about the New Testament prophet and prophecy. *The Happy Prophet* releases an impartation to live in joy, face the giant of fear, and walk in the revelation of the Father's love in both life and prophetic ministry.

Thanks, Keith, for writing books!! They are needed.

—Steve Backlund
Bethel Church, Redding, CA
Co-founder of Igniting Hope Ministries
Author of *Let's Just Laugh at That, Possessing Joy,* and others

My great friend, Keith Ferrante, writes with extreme vulnerability out of his own personal journey into what it means to live joy-filled. Keith taught me years ago how to allow myself to be loved by God in my emotions, and it freed me into encounters with the Holy Spirit at a level of joy that I never imagined possible. I embarked on a journey of encounters into intimacy, because through Keith, I discovered that joy is not tied to an event or circumstance; it is tied to a Person.

I have personally watched Keith walk out the journey described in this book. As you read *The Happy Prophet,* be prepared to encounter the anointing present here for life-transforming encounters with the Joyful One who will make your heart happy!

—Gary Hopkins
Vacaville, CA
Family Life Pastor, The Mission
Author of *Encounters With the Bridegroom*

Keith has crafted a much-needed narrative for the future flow of the Church. His desire to see prophets and prophetic communities healed and strong is very apparent and woven throughout this happy book. Gone are the days of gloomy and ill-humored prophets. If joy is our strength, then it should mark the prophetic call on all of our lives. *The Happy Prophet* will help frame the proper prophetic reference point and put joy center stage where it belongs.

—Brian Orme
La Jolla, CA
Co-Founder of Kingdomstrate
Author of *Jumpstart, Little Beans and A Big God, The Ascended Life,* and *Remember When*

The Happy Prophet is such a wonderful, completely transparent, and vulnerable look at how God brought Keith to a place of freedom, security, and sustained joy. It details how God wants to do the same with all of us. Keith is incredibly generous in sharing with us the good, the bad, and the ugly of his own personal journey.

The Happy Prophet will help equip upcoming emerging prophets with the understanding that our journey cannot be sustained without a foundation of joy. Keith is a passionate and authentic man, who wants to build a company of healthy prophets marked by love, joy, peace, and righteousness.

I highly recommend this book. I believe it will encourage you, challenge you, and knock the spirit of serious right out of you! *The Happy Prophet* is Keith's life message, and I am so honored to call him my friend.

—Rachel Carroll
Chicago, IL
rachelcarrollministries.com

The

Happy Prophet

The

Happy Prophet

"God's New Covenant Design For Prophets"

Keith B. Ferrante

Published by: EMERGING PROPHETS
Contact: admin@emergingprophets.com,
          EmergingProphets.com
Cover design: Shelby Gibbs, shel.bgibbs@gmail.com
Editing and interior layout: Creatively Inspired, LLC

Printed in the United States of America

Table of Contents

*This book is dedicated to
my lovely wife and children,
for whom I have labored
to present a more joyful
self that will ensure a
happier life together.*

Acknowledgments

I'm deeply appreciative to so many for their investment in my life that helped to shape *The Happy Prophet*. I'd especially like to thank the prophets and apostles who have believed in me for so many years:

- Dan McCollam, thank you for patterning a more joyful way in so many memorable instances, and for being such a great sounding board, mentor, and friend.

- Georgian Banov, thank you for presenting the New Covenant revelation that helped to establish sustainable joy within me.

- David Crone, thank you for mentoring some of the joyless behaviors right out of me.

- Wendell McGowan, thank you for fathering me in the Spirit so faithfully and for the great joy it released within me.

- Kris Vallotton, thank you for chipping off the rough edges and shaping me into a more useful vessel for the Kingdom.

- Steve Backlund, thank you for communicating such transformational mindsets that launched me into greater joyful experiences.

I'd like to thank Carol Cantrell for such an amazing job of editing and preparing this book for publication. What a timely gift you have been.

I'd also like to thank my amazing wife, Heather, who helped encourage me to move beyond discouragement and hopelessness and into a more joyful way of seeing things. You have been the greatest gift anyone could ever ask for. Your ever-present joy and constant love has made me more than I would ever be otherwise. I love you very much.

My greatest thanks is to Jesus Christ, of course, the happiest Prophet ever. Thank You for modeling the Father's love and His Word through Your Spirit in such a relentlessly happy gospel. I am joyfully Yours forever!

Foreword

Years ago, I read a statement that began transforming my personal life and my church paradigm. The statement said, "Distrust your religion if it is grumpy." Wow! That thought hit me like a slap in the face. What if I dared to gauge my religious success by the amount of joy I walked in? How successful would I be?

This brought up another question: Where did the Church ever get the idea that a somber, sober, grumpy demeanor somehow represented higher levels of holiness? Perhaps it came from viewing historic images of pastors and revivalists who rarely smiled. Maybe our sobriety was birthed from the serious and eternal nature of the business to which we are called. Perhaps the testimonies of believers laced with wearisome trials and tragic tribulations may have contributed to our grumpy journey. I even wondered if the many cares of this life were not weighing us down like every other sojourner on the planet.

Despite the many possible reasons for our grumpy religion, this one thing is certain: *In His presence is fullness of joy* (see Ps 16:11). Do you realize what that means? That fact clearly shows us that the holiest place in the universe is the happiest, most joyful place a person can ever be.

God is not grumpy, and neither should His followers be.

I first met the young, gifted and grumpy pastor named, Keith, over fifteen years ago. Keith impressed me right away with his intense passion for God and his longing for revival. This guy was wholly committed to God and His Kingdom. Yet, like most pastors I meet, Keith was profoundly frustrated. His struggle reminded me of a principle I had learned earlier in ministry, which states: Your greatest weakness is not the thing you are not good at, but rather, your greatest weakness is your strength overextended. That was my friend, Keith. He was so serious, so intense, so devoted, that he had sucked all the life out of his own journey. He was holy, but he wasn't happy.

I don't mean to imply in any way that Keith wasn't bearing good fruit. He certainly was. But my young pastor friend didn't know how, in that season, to enjoy the fruit he was producing or live in the pleasure of his own God-given productivity. How can we truly claim to be people of His presence if we don't manifest His joy?

Before meeting Keith, I had my own revolutionary joy transformation. I was the associate pastor who did water-only fasts for forty days, and prayed at least three times a day. I memorized huge portions of Scripture and gauged my spirituality by how well I performed for God. All those things are good in the proper place. But without seeking first the righteousness that comes only from God, all these forms of devotion and self-abasement were just filthy rags of self-righteousness. That was the state I was in when God encountered me with the joy of His unconditional love. In that season, I found myself so overwhelmed by the love and grace of God, that for the next seven years, people often described me as the town drunk (in the Spirit.) I was so undone by the depths of God's love for me that I often felt powerless to perform the many religious duties that had previously occupied my years of ministry. Like the priests in Solomon's temple who were overshadowed by the glory of the Lord, I could barely perform the "duties" of my priesthood. This seven-year season was my grumpy-religion detox. God had to get the performance-based religion out of me so I could do greater works from the pure stream of the love of God.

I interjected my own short story so that you will understand that when I met Keith, I recognized the place he had been living from. Over the next decade and a half, I witnessed Keith on his joyful journey. Together with his faithful wife and mentors, Keith began taking captive every grumpy thought and making it obedient to the knowledge of Christ's true nature. Keith became a joy-warrior, fighting his battles for, and from, the delight of true fellowship with the Holy Spirit.

Today, Keith stands as a joy-herald leading the way for a new breed of emerging prophets. No longer will the picture of a prophet be like the Old Testament somber naysayer with the pointy finger decreeing and declaring the wretched sins of the world to a hopeless people. The new breed of prophet points the finger heavenward to a God who spanned time, and space, and darkness, and sin, to restore glory, light, love, and truth to every hungry heart. These prophets are armed with the mightiest weapons of all—the power to displace every negative atmosphere with righteousness, peace, and joy in the Holy Ghost.

In *The Happy Prophet*, Keith presses past the typical joy-buzz and blessing-babble, digging his roots deeply into real-life issues and solid theology that make the joy-filled life a sustainable reality, not only for prophets, but for every sincere seeker. It's a good book and a worthy read. I feel privileged to testify as a character witness to the validity of his joy-journey. As a matter of fact, in the last few years, Keith has helped me remove a few stones from my own well of joy to keep those life-giving waters bubbling. I'm thankful for Keith, his journey, his transparency, and his friendship.

It is my hope and belief that *The Happy Prophet* will contribute to your own deliverance from any hint of grumpy religion into the depths of God's love with a joy unspeakable and full of glory.

—Dan McCollam
Co-Senior Leader, The Mission, Vacaville, CA
International Director of Sounds of the Nations
Author of *The Good Fight: Prophetic Processing Workbook, Prophetic Company, Basic Training For Prophetic Activation,* and others

Introduction

I grew up around prophetic ministers, though I didn't have a theological grid for their role in the church. I'm convinced my Grandpa Lewallen was a prophet. He worked at a psychiatric hospital for many years, and during that time he learned to execute deliverance, release healing, and witness many tangible demonstrations of resurrection power. I remember all the amazing stories he used to tell me of people who tried to kill him and the power of God always coming to his rescue to protect him. He told about patients in his ward getting saved and then brought back into their right minds. I heard stories of demons that visited his house, or the houses of other people, and what actions he took to get rid of them.

Prophets of Old

My grandfather's influences were Derek Prince, David Wilkerson, and others of a similar blueprint. My grandpa was not always an easy man to be around because of his strong temperament and being so set in his ways. Even still, for many years he was a primary influence that shaped me in the things of the Kingdom. He was a very disciplined man with well established times of fasting, prayer, and reading God's Word. Everyday he would wake up at five o'clock in the morning to pray for many people, read the Word, declare the promises of God, and joyfully worship. As a young child, I sat at his feet and learned so much from him, and that mentoring continued right on into my late twenties.

As I matured, however, I began to encounter my heavenly Father in other ways beyond what I had learned growing up in my home church. My grandfather had beliefs that I had wholeheartedly accepted when I was young until I began to see that a few of them didn't fully embody the heartbeat of a kind, heavenly Father, and the mindset Christ designed for us. For instance, when my grandfather witnessed to a person or encouraged them to return back to the Lord but they continued to resist the Lord and would die suddenly, according to my grandfather's beliefs, this person had simply "run out of God's grace." He believed that the person's untimely death was "the fear of the Lord" being demonstrated and this was all part of the prophetic ministry. I, too, experienced this type of "prophetic ministry" early on and one particular incident stands out vividly. A backslidden minister met with me and I spent our time together urging him to return back to the Lord. Unfortunately he did not yield to the Lord that night, and the very next day, he was killed in a car accident. To me at that time, it seemed to be a clear validation of my ministry to this man with a sobering reminder about resisting the prophetic voice of the Lord.

It wasn't until I met a mentor prophet, Kris Vallotton, that I realized that this prophetic ministry paradigm was not God's New Covenant design. That was an Old Covenant model, and I'm not even sure if it was ever God's design, but we definitely see it in operation in some of the prophets of old. But Jesus actually rebuked His disciples for wanting to operate in that kind of spirit.

> *And when his disciples James and John saw this, they said, Lord, wilt thou that we command fire to come down from heaven,*

and consume them, even as Elias did? But he turned, and rebuked them, and said, Ye know not what manner of spirit ye are of. For the Son of man is not come to destroy men's lives, but to save them. And they went to another village.

Luke 9:54-56, KJV

Kris helped me see that some of the old prophet ways I had picked up from my grandfather did not fit the New Covenant prophet. It took me some time to sort out the differences between my grandfather's views and this new mindset and standard I was learning. My grandfather was an amazingly faithful man who heard many accurate and useful words from the Lord that I honored, but who, like all of us, had a few beliefs that simply needed upgrading. I remember going to visit him once and mulling over in my mind the frustrations of our theological disagreements, when suddenly I heard the Lord say, "Son, I am pleased with your grandparents. They have done everything I have asked them to do. You go now and do what I've asked *you* to do."

Boom. Wow! The challenges with my grandfather were over. From that moment on I was able to just enjoy him and honor the valuable things he carried so powerfully without stumbling over the few areas of his biblical viewpoints I could not embrace.

A New Day, A New Way

I wrote *The Happy Prophet* to help paint a picture of a new day that I believe the Lord is inviting us into. This is certainly true for all those desiring to live a happier spiritual life, whether or not you are called into a prophetic ministry. Many of us have lived under a mixture of Old and New Covenant beliefs concerning the prophetic. We have misunderstood our role and how we are to be walking today under the New Covenant versus the ways of the Old Covenant prophets. Under the New Covenant, there is a new way of receiving prophets and a new way of executing prophetic ministry, and we will certainly explore these.

But my primary focus in this book is to lay out to emerging prophets the grid for which I believe every healthy prophet must operate, and that is, in **joy**. When I refer to "emerging prophets", I mean those who are not yet recognized as a prophet but are developing the gift and are being groomed for a day when they will prophesy from a healthy place and contribute well to the Body of Christ. I believe there are more prophets coming forth in this hour than ever before. Whether you are called to be a platform prophet, an intercessor prophet, a prophet to government, a prophet that speaks to those in the media or the business sphere, or a more hidden prophet, the need for internal development and maturity is the same. Yet with your specific prophetic assignment, a sign that the New Covenant has truly impacted you will be that you are overflowing with joy. In stark contrast to the stern-faced prophets of doom and gloom, in this hour, a company of prophets are emerging who exude the joy of Heaven and release it everywhere they go.

On a side note, when I use the term "prophets", I am referring to both male and female voices. Therefore, I may not use the term "prophetess" as often, only to simplify the text. The fact is, we see many examples of prophetesses throughout Scripture. I fully believe that both the male and female prophetic voices are as valuable and desperately needed today as they were historically.

My hope is that *The Happy Prophet* will provide some useful tools with its real-life examples as a model to encourage modern-day mature prophets, emerging prophets, and those who are pastoring prophets. So often I see prophets who carry beliefs, character, attitudes, fruit, and patterns of ministry that are incongruent to Jesus' New Covenant ministry design. If we are to be truly operating in the full power and authority afforded us, one of the most significant and obvious signs is that we will carry and release joy. Detailing what that looks like is one of the primary objectives of this book. I'll be addressing the prophet, identifying keys of the prophetic role and ministry, and laying out vital elements that help develop a happy prophet.

But first, let me begin by sharing my own personal journey into a lifestyle of joy.

From Serious
to Joyful

One

From the time I was a very young boy, I was passionate about the things of the Kingdom that I knew about. I was saved at age four, filled with the Spirit and speaking in tongues by seven, and by age eleven or twelve, I was having ecstatic encounters where I spoke in tongues all night at a Christian kid's camp. I was passionate and earnest about my faith. I led people to Jesus in the first and second grade, and brought my Bible to public school. I had the privilege of leading one young man to the Lord on the playground. He then got on the school bus that day and asked every child if they knew Jesus. My public teacher once sent me to the psychiatric counselor because she thought I was too "crazy" about Jesus. I was crazy, but not in a lost-mind kind of way. Jesus was everything to me! He's always been that to me. My parents would say, "Keith, you were just born that way."

I would often be found speaking in tongues in my prayer closet as a young boy, praying fervently. Through high school I continued to witness to people and lead them to Jesus, even right in front of the class. I would refute my teachers who claimed evolution was the way, and a time or two, I was even kicked out of the class for it. At the church where my dad pastored, I would often be found early in the morning praying before school with a few other students. I was truly hungry for the things of

God, and very serious about the business of the Kingdom. I was simply sold out to Jesus.

I had always planned to go to Bible College to be trained as a missionary, and so as soon as I graduated from high school, I flew two thousand miles away from home. After four years of Bible school, I received my license to preach. Instead of becoming a foreign missionary, however, God led me into other plans He had arranged for my early years. He wanted me to pastor a church right here in the U.S. so I could learn to love people well.

Now you may look at my history and think, *That's a pretty good history!* . . . and I agree. But I'm leading up to the part that needed upgrading.

During the time I was pastoring my church at the age of 23, I began to get a revelation of my inward state. It wasn't until I encountered spiritual fathers who carried the Father's kindness, as well as my own encounters with the heavenly Father Himself and His love nature, that I came to the realization, *I need some adjustments.*

Through these encounters I continued the same spiritual disciplines I had learned from my parents and grandparents and had started from early on into my pastoring years. I fasted days on end, prayed and worshiped fervently for hours and hours, read the Bible at set times, continued to witness earnestly as I always had, and preached with much zeal. But I began to notice that I didn't have much joy. *No joy? . . . how did this happen?* It wasn't evident to me until I saw some people who authentically carried joy. **You don't know you are missing out on something really important until you observe someone else with something you've never seen.** It's like tasting a tender rib-eye steak for the first time when you've been used to eating a difficult-tochew cheap steak your whole life. The revelation of it immediately raises the bar of possibilities. From that new vantage point, you know you will never return to where you were.

At first when I experienced genuine joy coming from a good Father towards me, I couldn't believe it. *He's happy with me. What? He's pleased with me . . . already? But I didn't do anything!* I just didn't get that. But that's how God was capturing me . . . with His pleasure.

I began to learn that God wasn't upset at me after all. He wasn't the God who was waiting to punish me, hurt me, heap on guilt, or worse, kill me. He was the God of *love*, who is enduringly patient, kind, and finds pleasure with me. *God is pleased with me.* It was beginning to sink in and have its transforming effect.

I was experiencing the genuine, authentic love of God directed towards me, and I knew I would never settle for less. We do not have to study the counterfeit in life; we only need to know the authentic. When training bank tellers to distinguish between an authentic and counterfeit dollar bill, they don't show them the counterfeits; they show them genuine dollar bills. When they get really familiar with them, they will be able to identify counterfeits easily. In the same manner, we need a revelation of the authentic where we will immediately spot the counterfeit. That season for me was where I discovered the authentic—a genuine spiritual life of God's personal acceptance and love—and it instantly exposed the counterfeit life I had been living in self-abasement, extreme self-denial, guilt, shame, and condemnation. By finding the real value of the Father's love poured out through Jesus to me, it contrasted what I had accepted as the norm up to that time—a perpetually unhappy state.

As my friend, Dan McCollam, often says:

> Distrust your religion if it doesn't make you
> happy.

I was certainly not happy; instead I was serious—way too serious. I was rarely secure that I was going to Heaven because my walk with God was in bad need of an upgrade into His love that brought joy. I had been living most of my life where I did not see God as pleased with me. But that was all changing as I began to experience His authentic love and pleasure apart from my rigid spiritual disciplines.

He was transitioning me into a new place of joy.

Upgraded From Joylessness

Two

You don't know what you don't know. I didn't know that joy was supposed to be a part of my normal experience until I ran into people who carried joy as a way of life. They carried it because they had caught something deeper— the Father's unconditional love.

How can you carry joy if you don't believe the Father is happy with you? I didn't. I lived with a belief that said, *I hope one day to get the 'well done, good and faithful servant' from the Father.* One day in my church parking lot in Willits, God whispered to me, "Son, I accepted you the day you gave your life to me at four years old, so why are you trying so hard to please Me?"

In that moment, I began to get a revelation that I was accepted; not just tolerated, but fully *embraced*.

How can you live with joy if you think Dad is mad at you? I didn't realize I had been living this way until He started revealing it. Much of the works I had done for Him for all those years had been unknowingly to earn His approval. I had been working hard to one day be welcomed into Heaven with a hearty, "Well done!" I didn't know that I didn't have to do works to get into Heaven. Now I could do works because I was *already* welcomed through Jesus. What He did for me was enough. If you don't know that simple but profound truth, then you live much of your life trying to win approval that is already yours. And that makes for such a joyless existence.

I was so serious—too serious—and uptight about many things. I would beat myself up for days over sermons I didn't feel I preached good enough. I would pray, fast, and repent over issues of manhood, feeling guilty over the normal God-given passions and desires of a man.

I didn't enjoy others or myself. I was extremely judgmental because I felt, if I wasn't easily accepted into Heaven, then certainly others weren't either. I felt it was my duty, then, as their pastor, to chisel away on the negative character and unholiness of others to get them ready for eternity and make sure they avoided the anger and wrath of God. After all, isn't that the role of a prophet?

I'm so glad God rescued me from all of that. I've taken the time to paint a picture of who I was so you would understand that this book was written from the place of one who's had to journey *out* of a serious and joyless existence. I'm not saying I've arrived completely, but I have found some keys along the way that have helped me learn to be a normal person first, and then a happy prophet.

What is a Prophet?

A prophet is one who speaks a word from the Lord and who has had to personally walk out that message in their own life. It doesn't mean they are the perfect picture of that message, it just means they have integrity and have applied its truth to their life. Therefore, a prophet *is* the message. He can't speak a message and then not genuinely live it. A teacher, on the other hand, can at times speak a message as if it is a concept that is separate from his or her personal reality. I used to do that. I would teach about each one of the gifts of the Spirit from a scriptural basis, but most of them I had not personally experienced.

I think it's kind of funny that Elijah was known as the one whose anointing would restore family.

> *See, I will send you the prophet Elijah before that great and dreadful day of the LORD comes. He will turn the hearts of the fathers to their children, and the hearts of the children to their fathers . . .*
>
> Malachi 4:5-6

Why was this so funny? God gave him a message about family, yet he was a loner with a rejection complex. Even still, God chose him to be the picture of one who would restore family, because He sees where we have come from, where we are, and where we are going. To bystanders, it may appear that our lives are not in sync with our message at times, but they don't know our history. I have seen prophets who carry messages where some doubt the authenticity of their word. But because I know a bit of the history of the one giving the word, I am aware that they actually have walked out every bit of the word that they carry and deliver. They may not be as natural at it as those more experienced, but when a prophet releases a word where they have personally flushed it out in their own life, it carries a powerful authority that has a profound impact upon its delivery.

Establish the Message Authentically

I am intentional about establishing this message of

joy as authentic in my life. It doesn't mean that I am the funniest and lightest guy out there. I have had to fight for every bit of it. But this message of joy has captured me.

Most of my ministry has bits and pieces of joy flowing through it. Some may wonder what the laughter is all about or the rambunctious praise, but for me, they are all pieces to this wonderful revelation that has captivated me. Joy is not just something that I *do* once in a while; it is who I am: **I am a carrier of joy.**

If joy is truly authentic to who you are, then it must be observable. It is like some people who *say* they are in love, while others *demonstrate* they are in love. James says it like this:

> But someone will say, "You have faith; I have deeds." Show me your faith without deeds, and I will show you my faith by my deeds.
>
> 2:18

In the same way, some people will say that they are carriers of joy but there is no outward demonstration that proves the truth of it. Now I am not judging what others do, but I have yet to find a person who has true joy where it doesn't leak out of his or her words, actions, and light up their face more often than not. Their joy expression may not appear as exuberant and energetic as some, but it should at least have discernible external effects. A wife would not feel loved, no matter how many times a husband told her he loved her, if he didn't demonstrate love through genuine affection, loving care, tenderness, acts of kindness, gifts, and physical outward expressions of his true inner feelings. Jesus demonstrated His love for us through a physical act of sacrifice on the cross.

> *But God demonstrates His own love toward us, in that while we were still sinners, Christ died for us.*
>
> Romans 5:8, NKJV

There was no question about His love. Just as carriers of love must be tangible, so, too, carriers of joy must have an outward evidence. One of the evidences is found in seeing the emotion of joy on someone. You see, two thirds of the Kingdom are emotions: joy and peace.

> *For the kingdom of God is not a matter of eating and drinking, but of righteousness, peace and joy in the Holy Spirit.*
>
> Romans 14:17

These emotions of joy and peace are not just something inward, theological, clinical, or positional. Hebrews tells us the basis for such tangible evidence we carry:

> *Fixing our eyes on Jesus, the pioneer and perfecter of faith, for the joy set before him he endured the cross, scorning its shame, and sat down at the right hand of the throne of God.*
>
> 12:2

There was nothing random or unknowable about what Jesus did. It was a public act, plainly seen by everyone present. His joy caused Him to go to the cross for us. His joy had an outward expression of sacrifice. It was His love for us that caused Him to have such joy, even in His excruciating suffering and death on the cross.

Love always concludes in joy.

When I like someone, I enjoy being around that person. The sign that someone likes me is the clear evidence they enjoy me. The sign that I am in love with God is joy. The sign that I am not being captivated by His love is when I choose to live somber, long-faced, and take life way too seriously.

But if I have truly discovered His love and acceptance, joy will be the natural result. That is why I didn't have much joy growing up. How could I? I didn't know I had a good Daddy who was happy and pleased with me. Once I settled that issue and began to experience His continual pleasure over me, I tapped into His ever-flowing river of joy. My serious life vanished. The joy didn't come all at once, mind you. His love had to saturate every part of my being and the joy came little by little. But it came . . .

The Joy Terminator

Three

One of the signs that you are not filled with joy is that you are deeply introspective. You can't have joy while ruminating negatively about yourself or current situations of concern, rousing your emotions into an unhealthy state.

Like I've said, I was a very serious believer. I mean, going to hell or making it to Heaven was no laughing matter, right? But I was missing the point. God did all the hard work so that I could enter into that place where He delighted over me because I was His great joy. Salvation is an experience, not just a theology. I had yet to know the joy of my salvation the Scripture speaks about.

> *With joy you will draw water from the wells of salvation.*
>
> Isaiah 12:3

Joy Flows Out

There should be a well that is within each one of us that flows out of us.

> *Whoever believes in me, as the Scripture has said, rivers of living water will flow from*

within them. By this he meant the Spirit, whom those who believed in him were later to receive. Up to that time the Spirit had not been given, since Jesus had not yet been glorified.

John 7:38-39

The Spirit of God living within us should be manifested to those around us. Whatever is seen on the outside is the reflection of what is within. If I have joy flowing outward, it is a sign of what is deeply established within me. For so many years I manifested seriousness. Why? I had a skewed view of how God viewed me personally and how He viewed humanity. I didn't know God was happy with me, but He is. He is not upset with me, or you, or humanity. In fact, I have even seen the Father laughing and dancing over me.

The Joyful One in You

I had always thought the Holy Spirit was the "easily grieved one." I began to see that this was not actually true. So one day, I asked the Lord for an upgraded view of the Holy Spirit. My first upgraded picture He gave was my prophet friend just laughing his head off and enjoying himself. In that moment, the Holy Spirit showed me that just as my friend was joyful, so, too, is the Holy Spirit joyful. Joy is His true nature. When you recognize the one who lives within you is happy, it will transform you from the inside out.

Nothing is sustainable unless you first realize that it is in God. The only way I know that a revelation can take me over is if I see it in God. When I see it in Him, then I know that it is in me. Why? Because I know I am a new creation and He lives in me.

42

> *It is no longer I who live, but Christ lives in me . . .*
>
> Galatians 2:20a

The fruit of having Christ in me is seen in the evidence of joy in my life and proof that this biblical truth is true.[1] Oh to simply accept the truth of the gospel! I learned that I don't have to *try* to be joyful. I just need to get a revelation of the joyful One who lives inside of me. He is a happy God, and *He lives in me.* His children—His offspring—have it in their DNA to reflect joy. As new creations, His nature is our nature. So joy is already there; we don't have to work it up because it is not our own joy, but His.

> *For the joy of the LORD is your strength.*
>
> Nehemiah 8:10b

The joy of the Lord fortifies all He is building within us. And *that* is a sustainable revelation.

Joy Terminators

So then, what are the greatest joy terminators? What are the things that come and steal our joy away? Lies from the enemy! He always likes to suggest Jesus didn't pay it *all* and we have a lot we still have to do to make God happy. We hear lies, such as:

- We are still part of the "old" creation (i.e., we're still under the requirements of Old Covenant);
- We are not enough (i.e., "we must do more!");
- *We* must carry *our* cross daily (as if to say, "Christ's death was not enough.").

---

[1] See 2 Cor 5:17, Gal 2:20, Gal 5:16.

You must do more!

People will use the words of Jesus to substantiate their point that we must do more works:

> *Then Jesus said to His disciples, "If anyone desires to come after Me, let him deny himself, and take up his cross, and follow Me."*

Matthew 16:24, NKJV

But what if this is more about carrying the revelation of His cross and what He already did for us?

Some support their argument with this verse of Paul's:

> *I die daily.*

1 Corinthians 15:31b, KJV

When Paul says, "I die daily," it is because he was potentially facing the reality of physical death on a daily basis; he was not saying he was trying to be good enough to come before God. To him, dying daily wasn't about beating himself up, but rather described what he was facing physically every day because of being persecuted for preaching the gospel. Being beaten and bruised, hiding out, and experiencing rejection were frequent occurrences for him. And yet, he spoke about joy in so many of his letters. How could he carry such joy? Because he had been captured by grace that he didn't deserve—grace he had previously so violently opposed. He had a revelation that he was the worst of sinners, but had been instead captured by God's kindness. It was this that led him to repentance. We, too, must get a revelation of God's infinite love for us to be led into the kind of sustainable joy that will endure through anything we face.

Here's the bottom line: If you don't have joy, question your theology and even the foundations of your faith.

Paul also said:

> *I want to know Christ—yes, to know the power of his resurrection and participation in his sufferings, becoming like him in his death.*

Philippians 3:10

What does he mean, "to know . . . His sufferings"? Does it really mean to suffer in this body, or could it mean to know what Jesus did for us in His sufferings? Is the focus of our spiritual walk all about our own personal self-sacrifice for Him? If Christ truly *finished* the work on the cross, then how is it we spend so much time and activity sacrificing our lives, believing we need to add to His perfect sacrifice? Paul made it pretty clear in his letter to the Ephesians:

> *For it is by grace you have been saved, through faith—and this is not of yourselves, it is the gift of God—not by works, so that no one can boast.*

2:8-9

I love that. Even the grace to be saved through faith doesn't originate from us. We didn't even get to take credit for the faith that got us in. It was *His* gift to us. So shouldn't we rather, *apply* the grace He provided through faith?

As I read this verse I see that faith is simply the gift of God. It is not our own abilities and efforts. Faith isn't even just a tangible thought we have. It is actually God Himself—it is the gift of God Himself to you. He is the reason we have entered into Heaven and can go into heavenly realities whenever we want to. He has gifted us

45

to be able to boldly approach His throne of grace at any time.

> *Therefore, since we have a great high priest who has ascended into heaven, Jesus the Son of God, let us hold firmly to the faith we profess. For we do not have a high priest who is unable to empathize with our weaknesses, but we have one who has been tempted in every way, just as we are—yet he did not sin.*
>
> *Let us then approach God's throne of grace with confidence, so that we may receive mercy and find grace to help us in our time of need.*
>
> Hebrews 4:14-16

We have a high priest who already entered that place. Jesus is our entrance, a gift God has given to us. That alone is our boast—not our efforts. Paul also says in Philippians:

> *What is more, I consider everything a loss because of the surpassing worth of knowing Christ Jesus my Lord, for whose sake I have lost all things. I consider them garbage, that I may gain Christ.*
>
> 3:8

Paul realized that everything he had ever done was equal to garbage, except for his embracing Christ. When I first received this revelation and began to walk it out, it questioned all my spiritual disciplines and why I did them. I had to honestly ask myself:

- What is my motivation?
- Why am I so hard on myself?
- Why am I so hard on others?
- Why do I have such a rigid standard?
- Why do I get so grieved over sin?

Yes, sin has consequences, but these are a result of sin's actions. The consequences of sin are never God-initiated.

> *For the wages of sin is death, but the gift of God is eternal life in Christ Jesus our Lord.*

> Romans 6:23

Sin's ultimate wages result in death; God's gift, however, is life—abundant life, in fact. Let's not confuse that. The Gospel of John reveals the essence and true heart of God the Father toward those He created:

> *For God so loved the world that he gave his one and only Son, that whoever believes in him shall not perish but have eternal life. For God did not send his Son into the world to condemn the world, but to save the world through him. Whoever believes in him is not condemned, but whoever does not believe stands condemned already because he has not believed in the name of God's one and only Son.*

> John 3:16-18

God's loving response to man's sin condition is in the person of Jesus, and through Him, full redemption and the abundance of eternal life.

Condemnation and punishment

So then, sin brings death—not God. He gives life. Condemnation or punishment is not God-initiated, but those who live in sin are subject to its domination and ultimate consequences.

Our job as New Covenant prophets is to have such a personal revelation of the New Covenant design that we minister to people out of that redemptive place where Jesus paid it all. There is simply nothing further we can add to His sacrifice on our behalf. But we can't minister from that place if we haven't first embraced it and reaped its fruit in our own lives. Here are some questions to help evaluate if you are truly living from that place of life and redemption.

- How much condemnation do you experience?

- How many negative thoughts about yourself do you live under?

- How much shame do you carry?

- Are you hard on yourself when you make a mistake?

- How many days does it take you to recover from words you should not have said, thoughts you should not have entertained, and actions you should not have expressed?

No matter the answers to these questions, go after an upgrade where you determine to live in the fully redemptive life already provided.

Wrong actions and thoughts

Now I know there is no excuse for wrong actions, because sin still has consequences. But we will never get out of the cycle of wrong thoughts and actions if we don't first recognize God breaks that cycle every time by offering us mercy and grace. Once we learn to come to Him instead of running away in shame, we will learn how to avoid the trap of sin and wrong actions. When we do fall short, He patiently walks us through the process of renewing our mind and we will begin to be more gracious to ourselves in those times because we truly believe we are a new creation. We can then make this declaration with confidence: **As a new creation, I am prone to do what is right and good; left to myself I *will* make the right decision.** The more we live in this truth, the more we will find kindness and mercy flowing generously out of us toward others.

Remember this, **you can only give away what you possess.**

An Upgraded View of God's Immeasurable Nature

When you give away the "anger" of God, it is a sign that you are still seeing God as angry. That only means you need an upgraded view of how God views you. Ask Him for that. Because what you perceive as His view towards you is what you are currently communicating and releasing to others.

Determine to increase your momentum of maturity as a happy prophet overflowing with His joy with a fresh revelation of the immeasurable patience of our God. He is always revealing His nature to you, so see Him as the one who is incredibly patient with *you*. This elevated view of God will unlock His joy even more in you and will establish your journey more and more as a happy prophet.

The Foundation
of Happy
Prophets

Four

For a long time my view of God was that He was always angry, always serious, and rarely smiled. Isn't that how we often viewed the prophets of old as they delivered the message of God to the people? Because the New Covenant includes the prophetic office right along with apostles, it would be good to study the characteristics and distinctions between the Old and New Covenants.

First off, what is the placement of apostles and prophets?

> *Built on the foundation of the apostles and prophets, with Christ Jesus himself as the chief cornerstone.*

> Ephesians 2:20

I used to think it was only the apostles who saw Christ and prophets were on a lesser plane. But here we see both apostles *and* prophets are established on equal terms upon one foundation, which is Christ.

I believe Barnabas functioned in both as a prophetic apostle, but he was first a prophet. He is a picture of a healthy New Covenant prophet because he is particularly known for encouragement.[2] Bringing encouragement to the Body of Christ is especially important for those who

---

[2]   See Acts 4:36-37.

hold the office of prophet and is not just reserved for those utilizing the gift of prophecy.

A New Lens

The Old Covenant prophet's behaviors and beliefs must be viewed through the lens of the New Covenant in order to determine what is proper New Covenant protocol and what isn't. For instance, acting like Elijah and calling down fire from Heaven upon resistant villagers isn't what we do. Jesus reprimanded His disciples for suggesting such an action and instructed them that it was the wrong spirit.

We see many examples of God's mercy toward people in spite of the prophet's bias or temperament. God demonstrated His heart of compassion towards Nineveh after they repented, but Jonah did not. He was angry that God did not bring the judgment he prophesied.

Moses was kept out of the Promised Land because of his angry attitude. I have learned that if you have anger in your heart, you will see the signs of anger and wrath manifest around you and they will emerge in your message. But that doesn't mean it reflects the nature of God. It means, what is in your heart will follow you.

There are many Old Covenant prophet actions that are incompatible under the New Covenant design.

Let's look at an action by Peter. What if Ananias and Sapphira's death wasn't a validation of the Holy Spirit's New Covenant ministry but what was the Old Covenant thinking still resident in Peter's heart?

> *Then Peter said to her, "How is it you have agreed together to test the Spirit of the Lord? Look, the feet of those who have buried your husband are at the door, and they will carry*

you out.

Acts 5:9, NKJV

Luke, the author of the Book of Acts, is writing word-for-word what Peter said, but it doesn't mean we prophets need to follow this example. Instead, we should take into account that it wasn't too long prior to this incident that Peter adamantly told Jesus:

> *Even if I have to die with you, I will never disown you.*

Mark 14:31

And yet, that same night he denied he even knew Jesus. Clearly, Peter was in training and still sorting out the distinctions of the Old and the New with the Holy Spirit. It is vitally important to question where we get some of our reasoning for judgment and wrath and make adjustments.

Emerging Models of Happy Prophets

I love the prophets I am seeing emerge today. People like Shawn Bolz, Heidi Baker, Jerame Nelson, along with many others, deliver a message of grace and mercy to the Body of Christ and the lost. They are good models of a New Covenant prophet carrying New Covenant language direct from the heart of the Father. While they each have unique ministry styles, the message from their hearts rings true. I'm not suggesting that everything in their message is perfected or accurately delivered in a New Covenant manner. I would say that we all—including myself—are on a journey to develop the language and tone of a good and loving Father.

I have had the privilege to be around a number of prophets for many years now, and I have observed that some are still carrying a residual of the Old Covenant in their speaking and thinking. They are faithfully carrying and delivering His message according to their revelation. But in this next season, God is bringing forth those who will take it further: A company of prophets is emerging who live and breathe the finished work of Jesus.

I believe New Covenant prophets need the revelation of New Covenant apostles. I have fed off the teachings and personal encounters I have had with Georgian and Winnie Banov for the last 14 years or so. They carry the message of the finished work of Jesus powerfully—what every New Covenant prophet should also be carrying. I have heard a few leaders offhandedly comment about the Banov's ministry with their festive lighthearted-joy, that such joy is just too hard to manage in a "normal" church. I disagree. The joy the Banov's carry is very intentional and potent, and is a direct outflow from their intimate relationship with Jesus. In fact, every believer needs to embrace a radically joyful, grace-filled, good view of the Father.

The Message of "Glad Tidings"

We have a challenging mandate that requires us to be joyful advocates of the gospel as we deliver His message prophetically to the nations.

> *And the gospel must first be preached to all nations.*

> Mark 13:10

The Greek word for "gospel" is translated in English as "glad tidings".[3] The glad tidings message is the happy gospel.

---

[3] Strong's Greek Concordance, #G2097, *"euaggelizó"*.

We have to get this: God is not mad at the world. Rather, He is commissioning us to present this glad reconciliation message to the nations.

> *That God was reconciling the world to himself in Christ, not counting men's sins against them. And he has committed to us the message of reconciliation.*

2 Corinthians 5:19

The Ministry of Reconciliation

What's even greater than personally receiving reconciliation? Carrying the message of reconciliation and giving it away every chance we get. This is not an option for the believer, but rather, it is our primary message and ministry.

"Come to God." That's a big one. Is it, "Come to God all cleaned up"? No, it's, "Come to God *as you are.*" He's the one who will get you all cleaned up. When you see His purity, you don't want to live under filth any longer. When you see how He treats people, you will be called up higher.

Slow to Anger

I remember when I began to get a revelation that He is a gentle, patient God. I saw in Scripture that it took Him a good four hundred years to get mad. I was undone. I had to read the Bible from a different lens to come to that conclusion. Many Bible translations translate the word for "patient" or "longsuffering" when referring to God's character as "slow to anger." What if we saw God as someone who is "slow to dilate the nostrils," as described in one Hebrew definition of "slow to anger"[4]? That seems to suggest that God's personality leans a bit on the angry side. It would be like saying, "He is an angry God, but it takes a while for His anger to manifest." And that's how I understood it.

But I love The Message Bible's translation of this verse about God's character:

> God passed in front of him and called out, "God, God, a God of mercy and grace, endlessly patient—so much love, so deeply true—loyal in love for a thousand generations, forgiving iniquity, rebellion, and sin."
>
> Exodus 34:6, MSG

This translation does not portray anger as a normal manifestation or typical of God's personality at all. Could it be that we have misunderstood God's response to the activities of man and we must learn to see instead that His primary characteristic is "endlessly patient"? He is actually a kind, gentle, and loving God. And this is the very nature of God the Father we saw reflected in Jesus.

> A bruised reed he will not break, and a smoldering wick he will not snuff out, till he has brought justice through to victory.
>
> Matthew 12:20

God is not the type of person to break people. Neither should we, His prophets. We are intended to be a reflection of the person He is, just as Jesus reflected the Father. If we are not reflecting Him, then who are we reflecting? We could be emulating someone else but attaching God's

---

4   Strong's Hebrew Concordance, #H639, "har-af".

name to our actions. There is power in what and who we are reflecting, so we must walk carefully.

This is not to say that God doesn't get upset or that we won't ever respond in anger; it is a human emotion, after all. But it is what we do with it that matters. We have this biblical exhortation:

"Be angry and do not sin . . ."

Ephesians 4:26a, NKJV

Clearly there are times when anger may be present, but it shouldn't be the normal response and expression that emerges every time we encounter something we disagree with. I have to admit that isn't always easy when I'm functioning as a prophet. Sometimes you're tempted to be angry when you feel people aren't catching what you believe to be the word of the Lord. Sometimes, it seems to take way too long for people to embrace what God is telling them. And sometimes it takes years before they finally start seeing what you are seeing and even longer to apply that truth.

By demonstrating a "slow to anger" attitude, however, and choosing to make it our default, we are exemplifying the prophetic gift, and thereby magnifying the true nature of God.

Upon this Foundation

In such times, I see the one who is endlessly patient, and it fills me with the desire to be more and more like Him. As New Covenant happy prophets, presenting the "glad tidings" in the tone of our loving Father is our primary focus, and only possible because of our intimacy with Jesus. Let's continue to develop that.

Joyful Patience

Five

I pastored my first church in Willits, California, for ten years, and I loved the people there. I really did. On occasion I admit I was frustrated with the normal things that frustrate pastors. Sometimes it seemed like a few of the people I pastored resisted the changes I saw as necessary for maturity. Despite these frustrations, I learned the journey wasn't really about them changing but more about *me* changing. Unfortunately, I didn't see then what I know now. At that time, I just wanted everyone to change . . . and right away! To me, that would be the sign that my ministry was effective. Well, as you can imagine, I have had to let go of that pipe dream again and again. The fact is, change takes time.

When I left the pastorate to move to Vacaville, California, my wife observed a significant change in me. After a year or so of not pastoring a church full time, she observed the gentler side of me begin to emerge once again.

"There you are," Heather told me one day. "There's the real Keith again." She had lost parts of me during the pastorate. I had become so frustrated in preaching the same message over and over because I wasn't seeing the results. That's one sign of being a prophet—one message per season. It doesn't mean a prophet can't preach other messages; it's just at certain times they are meant to be specifically focused on one particular message.

For instance, in my church, it seemed that some had a hard time applying the biblical principles of generosity and faithfulness in giving. Those who had a habit of gossiping did not apply the message to be gracious with their words. Some who had been wounded by people in authority had a difficult time learning to trust the leaders God gave them. And so, I would preach my message again and again, and this only created more frustration in me.

It's His Message

One of the things I was attempting to learn at that time was to accept people as they are. I came to realize that the words God gave me to speak ultimately were His— not mine. It wasn't even my responsibility whether people matured, changed, or stayed the same. I was responsible to be faithful to deliver the message He gave me for them. I was learning to just be a postman delivering the mail from Heaven.

I began to see this same pattern happen as I pastored the youth group at the church where I ministered a few years ago. At one particular time, I was especially going after purity being restored in our youth and not realizing that once again, I was wearing the prophet's hat—the one who will sound the same gong over and over until the word is received or rejected. If it is rejected and a prophet hasn't matured sufficiently, they may leave the church feeling personally rejected, or they will simply switch to another message.

Once I realized that I was doing the same thing I had done while pastoring in Willits, I got a revelation that I didn't have to stay in the same frustrated place as a prophet as I did before. The Lord showed me that I was *carrying* a word. Not seeing quick results from a prophetic word in your immature state can tempt you to anger. I came to realize that I had spoken the word already for several months and it was now time to let the seed rest in the soil of the hearts of the youth and move on to something else. But it is sometimes hard for a prophet to do that. I had to learn that I was not grieving God when I let a word rest that is not readily being received or immediately implemented. This is where joyful patience is worked in the prophet.

The joy came after I made this decision to let it rest. Over time, I observed several of the youth really catch that word of purity and begin to run with it. This is the reward of patience as you discover God is working amongst those to whom you faithfully delivered the word.

Burning with Revival Fire

I noticed this same tendency to get impatient and angry surfacing again in another way. I had been doing a study on the prophets, and one day, the Lord told me to study John the Baptist. As I did, I realized John was like a revivalist. I pictured him living in modern times looking like Steve Hill, the prophetic evangelist of the Brownsville Revival.[5] I got on YouTube and watched the video of Steve's recent funeral. As I heard the life and legacy of Steve, I received an impartation that night of the John the Baptist mantle. *I was burning with holy fire!* I was up much of that night processing this revelation. That next morning at church, someone asked me to do the transition for the Sunday morning service. This is the

---

[5] Brownsville Revival, Brownsville, Florida, 1995.

portion of the service where you take a few minutes and help the congregation move from the worship time into the announcements.

I told them, "Look, I'm burning with this revival spirit . . . you should probably find someone else to do that!"

"No, go ahead Keith," came their answer, "we really need your voice this morning."

At the end of our worship time, I walked up onto the platform, and sure enough, the burning fire of revival erupted right out of me. I went on and on for about 15 minutes—way longer than normal for a transition—and someone eventually came up to take back the meeting because of the tight schedule that morning. But I was completely engulfed with the burning fire of that revival spirit! I was simply unable to function on any "normal" level, and certainly not according to that morning's agenda!

Later on, my wife suggested that I take that revival passion burning inside of me and direct it in our dedicated prayer room. I did just that and called some other friends to join me also in prayer. We met every night for 40 nights. About 15 days in, I noticed that the passion I was carrying for revival, purity, coming back to God, etc., was causing me to get more and more agitated with some of the people at the prayer meeting and even at some not attending. You see, when you are carrying a standard, without realizing it you sometimes begin to judge others with your limited perceptions about their internal changes or lack of them.

Like John the Beloved

It was then that the Lord said to me, "Keith, I want you to study up on another prophet and apostle, John the Beloved." It wasn't too long after I did that study that I caught his spirit, too. I caught the spirit of love for Jesus and people all around me. I was in love, and it just poured out of me. My impatience left in an instant, and the grace and mercy returned.

It was then that the Lord said, "Keith, you need to carry both Johns in your spirit." The spirit of John the Baptist on its own can lead to criticism and judgmentalism, while the spirit of John the Beloved on its own can lead to unsanctified lenience or sentimentalism. We need the combination of both of those truths working in union together to carry us through into a mature state.

We must learn how to speak the truth in love; we need both grace *and* truth.

> *For the law was given through Moses; grace and truth came through Jesus Christ.*

John 1:17

If we just have the truth, we will be prophets like Peter where our zealous immaturity will respond rashly and cut off ears instead of heal hearts. Paul said he was given a ministry to build up rather than to tear down.

> *This is why I write these things when I am absent, that when I come I may not have to be harsh in my use of authority—the authority the Lord gave me for building you up, not for tearing you down.*

2 Corinthians 13:10

Deliver the Message Again . . . and Again

It is a special challenge and has some pitfalls even when you are delivering the same message to the same group of people but seeing little results. My friend, Dan McCollam, says that when it doesn't seem like your words are being heard, wait a few months and then deliver the same message a different way. Then wait a few more months and try communicating your prophetic concept another way. After a while, it may be that it then settles in, and those for whom the word was intended will be changed and begin to walk in it.

I have had to learn that, and I have also had to learn to disconnect the prophetic reception of the word I deliver from my own personal identity. If I felt like the word was not being received, I would respond with a bit of frustration. When frustration develops because of people's lack of receptivity, the words I release will be tinged with anger because it feels like a *personal* rejection—like they are against *me*. I feel because they don't want the prophetic word, they don't want *me*. It is at this point I realize that I have made His message and its acceptance personal. I tie their inability to receive me/the word to my identity as God's child: *I am not being received.* This lie of the enemy *always* gets me in trouble. The key for me is to identify when I have allowed His word to become *my* word, and have taken their response I perceive as rejection, personally. Once I identify this, I can take appropriate action to speak truth and counter the lie. *Boom.* The joy is back.

To prevent this cycle from ever developing in the first place, there are two things I keep in mind. First, the hearers of the prophetic word will eventually receive it and walk in the word **if I am patient and wise in delivering it.** And secondly, **I must believe that I am received.** I can't live and minister with a rejection complex. But even if those who hear the word don't receive me, I still have to believe the truth.

> *What, then, shall we say in response to this?*
> *If God is for us, who can be against us?*

> Romans 8:31

Walking in our Primary Identity

That is the truth I choose to believe: *God is for me. I am His son.* I have to live under that. My primary identity is not, "I am a prophet." My primary identity is, "I am a son and I am His Bride. I am His beloved and He is mine. I am loved unconditionally." Therefore, I can never allow people's responses to my ministry or ministry style or even the message I deliver in any way affect the favored position I hold in God's heart and His love and passionate affections toward me. I really do believe that *nothing* can separate me from the love of God[6]—especially not the opinions of man. That truth is something I must repeatedly acknowledge when communicating a word of the Lord.

Joyfully "Constant" Forerunners

Prophets are often a bit ahead of where everyone else is. God made them that way. They see the future; they see what's up ahead. They see what God wants to bring on the

---

[6] See Rom 8:39.

earth and they are captured by the reality of the revelation of God's new day about to dawn. Prophets sometimes think the word is meant for now, but often it is not. They are called, instead, to speak it into existence. They are to walk, at times, as a forerunner of a word until it is caught and built into the lives of the people for whom it was intended, as well as follow through in implementing the support structures within organizations. If the prophet doesn't realize that being a forerunner is a part of his or her life, then they will be limping along in the race instead of joyfully persevering in the journey as God intends.

> *Therefore, since we are surrounded by such a great cloud of witnesses, let us throw off everything that hinders and the sin that so easily entangles. And let us run with perseverance the race marked out for us.*

> Hebrews 12:1

The word "persevere"[7] in the Greek means to be "joyfully constant". The pursuit of the prize of the high calling in Christ[8] is meant to be a joyfully consistent one. There is always more to go after in the Kingdom, and so, we must know how to run the race joyfully constant with ever-increasing patience in order to endure to the end.

---

[7] Strong's Greek Concordance, #G5281, *"hupomoné"*.
[8] See Phil 3:14.

Wise in Warfare

Six

I think it is important to explore what can take us unexpectedly out of the race. Not knowing what might be hidden deep inside can cause us to be sideswiped by the enemy in our pursuit of more of God.

Elijah is one of my favorite prophets. We all love the exploits of this particular prophet, but are also sobered by his moments of weakness. We realize that we, too, can experience a similar weakness if we don't have wisdom and understanding well established to guide us.

I love the fire that prophets have. It is especially great to be around a company of emerging prophets that are burning with passion for the Kingdom of God. I have been privileged to be with many of these in a variety of situations where I observe them growing stronger, more passionate, and more effective in their Kingdom pursuits.

One thing that I see all too often as people catch a bit of the passion of God is that they begin to recklessly run at the enemy with their newfound revelation. It reminds me of myself a few years back.

Incautious Warfare

In the early days when I was just learning spiritual warfare tactics and wisdom's lessons of what to do and what not to do in prophetic acts and intercession, I went to Brazil with some fired-up friends. We visited the famous Christ the Redeemer statue that overlooks Rio de Janeiro. I had no idea what I was going to find as we all stood at the base of that statue. The monument that towers 125 feet above the city for all to see also had a shrine to Mary at its base, which according to legend had been brought from the bottom of the river. It didn't seem fitting that at the base of the statue of Christ there stood an idol. As visitors streamed up the mountain for a closer view of Christ the Redeemer, they had to pass by an attendant safeguarding this idol at its base, and many spontaneously offered a monetary donation. I sensed the oppressive spirit so thick there, and I felt myself growing more and more irritated, as did some of those with me. We soon began to rattle off some rapid fire rebukes at that residing oppressive spirit, and it wasn't long before I began to feel the after-effects of this action. It occurred to me that I hadn't even asked the Lord if I was supposed to deal with that spirit, done with a bit of arrogance, I might add. It wasn't that I didn't have authority; it was that I was dealing with that spirit in a presumptuous reviling manner. A good month of backlash followed me home after this incident that left me with a distressed and tormented mind which permeated the atmosphere. I soon recognized what happened, repented, and pulled out of it.

Another time I took a team on a prayer walk along the coast of California, something I do from time to time. As we were walking along, I confronted specific evil spirits that I knew were resident there. There were signs and wonders that verified our effectiveness, but we also experienced backlash for about a month afterwards. There was even the death of a key member that we knew was directly related to our warfare on that intercessory walk, and other team member's experienced serious retaliation as well—discouragement, heaviness, etc.

God was teaching me something very important at that point and He had my full attention. I knew I was destined to do even greater prophetic acts and intercessory walks in the future, but He wanted it done the right way. He directed me to this section in Jude:

> Yet Michael the archangel, in contending with the devil, when he disputed about the body of Moses, dared not bring against him a reviling accusation, but said, "The Lord rebuke you!" But these speak evil of whatever they do not know; and whatever they know naturally, like brute beasts, in these things they corrupt themselves.
>
> vs 9, 10, NKJV

It wasn't that I didn't know *how* to deal with the enemy; it was the *manner* in which I did it. I had confronted him with a slanderous and arrogant attitude. This was an important but hard lesson to learn.

Since that time, I have been on many "joy" walks. God taught me: "Keith, I gave you weapons of praise and joy as well as the strategy of enjoying the companions with whom you're ministering." It wasn't that God didn't intend for me to take territory; it was *how* I needed to do it. His course of action is always best. That was key, and that is the wisdom we must learn.

Elijah had the same issue. He found himself confronting false prophets, but he did it with a bit of arrogance.

> *At noon Elijah began to taunt them. "Shout louder!" he said. "Surely he is a god! Perhaps he is deep in thought, or busy, or traveling. Maybe he is sleeping and must be awakened."*

1 Kings 18:27

It wasn't long after this incident that we see Elijah running for his life out of *fear* of Jezebel. When you taunt the enemy in such a way, it becomes an open door allowing him to find any cracks in your foundation (i.e., fear, rejection, unhealed woundedness, etc.) and exploit it, using it against you. That's why we must always utilize the authority we have in Christ when facing off with the enemy, and not run at him in a haughty manner, flaunting our power. If we move against him in our own strength, we *will* face the consequences and squander our joy. I'm not trying to instill fear, but I definitely want to encourage you to walk wisely in warfare.

Those who carry out spiritual warfare by reviling the enemy will do so at the expense of their joy, because it is going to be assaulted. Jezebel struck back at Elijah with a spirit of fear through intimidation. Fear shuts down power, whereas love casts out fear. Elijah did not have a full measure of victory going on in his life. The hidden cracks in his internal foundation of rejection, loneliness, and believing he was the only one serving God, were quickly revealed. Those are the quickest joy thieves. As Elijah ran out of fear for his life following his presumptuous slandering of the demonic realm, all his joy dissipated.

Walk in Humility

Countless times I've seen people ascend a mountaintop to do spiritual warfare. They are energized at making a Kingdom-advancement in a territory where they have passion. Suddenly, the enemy targets old wounds from a father, mother, leaders, brothers, sisters, bosses, etc. In just a few moments, they are completely taken out of the battle—until they can get healed, that is. I love using these moments to help people get free of those long-held strongholds. It's not always easy, but it's so worth it. The following story illustrates this.

I was with about 20 people on a high point in Ireland. We were finishing ten days of climbing four mountains in the UK. We had seen a lot of breakthrough with signs and wonders. It was great! But as we neared the top of the last mountain, the enemy attacked head-on. Several of our team members held hidden wounds, and just at that strategic moment, they became targets of the enemy. These wounds turned into verbal attacks against my leadership and other team members:

- "You're not a good leader."

- "People don't care for me."

- "I'm not going any farther!"

I knew right then and there that this was spiritual warfare 101: The enemy waits until we are just about to attack his stronghold and then pinpoints those hidden areas of agreement with his stronghold in the hearts of team members. He accesses them in order to disempower us in an attempt to stop us dead in our tracks. I had developed enough wisdom by then to properly identify this direct assault against our leadership team for what it was: spiritual warfare. It's not always easy to address such issues when your leadership is being targeted specifically. You must respond in humility and go after the spirit behind the attack.

With this in mind I said to them, "You may think I am like your father that hurt you, but I am not that person. I am not going up to the mountaintop without you alongside of me. Let's go after the healing of your heart. Then we will ascend all together." We stopped our expedition up that mountain and waited until God healed each person. Only then did we ascend the rest of the way up together. The fruit that occurred in that nation following this intercessory walk was tangibly evident. It was worth the effort of pressing all the way through.

Walking in humility and leaning on Jesus every step of the way is key to going the distance. I know that when I enter a new nation or new territory, I will often discover something I have not faced before. Sometimes it brings up an issue in my life that I need to deal with. But when I am walking in humility instead of overconfidence, then I can trust God won't lead me to a place I can't walk through victoriously. That is where sustainable joy comes. The enemy can only go after the wounds in our heart that we refuse to admit we have because of pride.

I know that I am healed and healthy in Christ, but there are still upgrades that I haven't yet discovered in Christ's victory for my life. Sometimes I see people in a corporate meeting manifesting laughter and joy and it is clear they are having a great time. They confidently and publicly talk about joy and minister in joy. But sometimes that joy is not established on healthy foundations. The test is not whether you can laugh in a corporate meeting that determines your maturity, it's whether you can laugh in the midst of a trial that tests your genuine maturity.

I remember having returned back home after being

out ministering for a long while and I was in one of our church staff meetings. I was a bit grumpy that day and even had my arms crossed to show I was pretty miserable as the staff meeting dragged on and on. One of my leaders finally looked at me and said, "Keith, how is it that you can minister with such joy in the public meetings you lead but you can't manifest joy here at home? Is the joy in you really authentic?" Ouch, that hurt. But I needed it. I needed to be called up.

If joy is genuine, I need to be able to access it even in situations where I don't fully enjoy everything that is going on at that moment.

Joy in Trials

Seven

Learning to utilize the New Covenant weapon of joy in every situation is essential. As prophets we have to make sure we're not using any tools outside the finished work of Jesus. If we are, we may be empowering evil spirits who will seek to harm us.

Anyone can have joy in the midst of sweet victories when life all around us is peaceful and nice and as pleasant as summer sunshine. But sustainable joy is primarily birthed in trials.

You sure you want to keep reading?

No more Serious Faces

As prophets, God desires us to be a demonstration of Heaven. As we see what is going on in Heaven, we are then to be a living word manifesting that reality. With that said, I believe every prophet should also physically manifest joy. No longer should the facial expressions of the prophet's delivery be marked by seriousness, somberness, anger, sorrow, and sadness, so as to be regarded as "normal."

That's not us. Joy is supposed to be an integral part of the New Covenant happy prophet.

I am thankful for my wife, my kids, and some of my

emerging prophet friends, who will from time to time remind me to smile. My wife will at times tap my forehead in an attempt to relax my crunched-up brow from its fixed serious demeanor. Do you ever lie down in bed at night and suddenly realize that you have been frowning for a long time, or your fists are clenched up tight? You don't even know how long you were set in that serious tense position. We really do have to learn to "let go and let God."

Trials Challenge the Promise

One of the challenges about trials is that it tests the best of us.

Prophets want results. They see what God is doing and they know what is available. The challenge is, when the promise hasn't yet manifested, the trial period begins. Between the prophecy and the promise fulfilled is the trial. Prophets are great at prophesying and seeing things in the Spirit, but their authority is tested, established, and built in the time of trial.

A number of years ago I went through an especially difficult season. It seemed like everything was coming against me: finances were tight, relationships were tense, and I was in the bottleneck before the breakthrough. But I had received a word from the Lord before everything started coming at me: "Keith, you are going to go through a season of accusation. When you learn joy in the process, I'll remove the accusation and increase the anointing on your life." That season was two years of being falsely accused, watching my church shrink, experiencing leaders in my church movement coming against me, and much more. Needless to say it was not a pleasant time.

But God was teaching me joy through it all, and eventually He brought the anointing increase through a minister who prayed over me. After that prayer, the trial ended, the accusations ceased, the leaders apologized, and there was a stronger dose of joy that was well established and resident in my life.

Don't Give In, Don't Give Up

Trials come, but then joy increases. We *always* win if we stay in the game and don't give in to discouragement.

In difficult or discouraging times, I'm so thankful when my wife, Heather, will find ways to activate me back to joy by suggesting I listen to some happy music or jump around a little and dance, or even watch a funny movie. Sometimes we just need to physically move our bodies to break heaviness.

I remember once I was so discouraged about the season I was in, I could only lay in my bed. I just couldn't get out. I was depressed and very low over an incident. That sounds a bit like Elijah. I was simply stuck in that place feeling really discouraged, and saying, "Oh what's the use, God?" And that's exactly how I felt. I had to actually have someone come by who believed in the power of praise, and he literally roared and shouted praise over me until that spirit of discouragement lifted. I was then able to get out of bed.

I was in another season where heaviness and discouragement just would not lift. Except in this season, if I got out of a depressed spot one day, it was back the very next day. If I spent a couple hours praising, the heaviness returned an hour after I finished. Nothing seemed to work.

Activate a Joy Lifestyle

But I knew God was activating a *lifestyle* of joy in my life. You see, we were given the gift of joy in Christ, but what we get to offer back to God is a larger portion of joy than we received at first. We receive a seed of joy in the Holy Spirit, and then we get to return a basketful of ripe and juicy joy-fruit right back. That only comes by remaining joy-filled—especially in the depths of trials. When we bear the fruit of joy in the midst of our deepest trials, we can expect our greatest reward.

Trials are the weights used when you are developing strength in the exercise of joy. How are you supposed to get a stronger joy-anointing if you have no resistance training? In the midst of it all, however, we must remember that God is so good, and He will never allow more than we can handle.

Just start laughing

Well, at this particular time, I was in a *season* of trials. It didn't matter how much I laughed, I was gloomy the next day. One day, my brother Paul posted some videos on social media of Kenneth Hagin meetings where he was laughing and the whole room was getting hit with that joy. I started watching them and I, too, got hit with that joy—right in my house. I was just blasted and drunk in the Spirit. That was so wonderful! Except, when the drunken joy lifted, there I was again, wrestling with discouragement.

But then I began to war with the joy. I used whatever I could to ignite my heart. Sometimes you have to throw a little joy-water down into your well if you want to get a spring of joy-water to bubble up.

Whoever believes in me, as the Scripture has said, rivers of living water will flow from within him." By this he meant the Spirit . . .

John 7:38-39a

That means, at times you have to steward the joy already resident within, which is the Holy Spirit. So I began to do that.

Praise is Heaven's tongue

Most people who speak in tongues believe that they can speak in tongues whenever they want to; most people also believe they can praise spontaneously. You know that you can start singing songs of praise or speaking in a heavenly language and before too long, you'll get caught up in the river of heavenly encounters. Well, the same goes for joy! **Joy is a place in God.** God *is* joy, and joy is present in the atmosphere all around Him.

In Your presence is fullness of joy . . .

Psalm 16:11, NKJV

So if you want to get into God's presence, find joy and activate it. Start laughing, start thanking Him; it's a quick way into the throne room.

Some people get into God's presence through an environment of peace and soaking. However it works for you, just get in. But there are other times when you just can't get a victory without the emotion of joy being activated. It is a major weapon of spiritual warfare that really works!

Deal fear a death blow

I remember I was doing a joy-walk at the coast west of Willits where I was living. I was in a season of dealing with fear. Fear will render you powerless, which will then deactivate your joy. But we know that love drives fear away, and along with love comes joy. It's the reward of those who know God loves them.

Well, here I was stuck in a cycle of fear. A mentor of mine told me I needed to just put on a jester's hat and dance like a fool through those seven coastal cities where we were doing a prayer walk. He said that I needed to get it settled in my heart that I was a fool for the King and no one else's. So I did that. I went laughing, and dancing, and leaping like a fool through those seven cities. Of course, it wasn't without resistance, and not without a few heads turning away in disgust. I even had a few people cuss me out along the way. But, oh what a joy!

Those were not easy times for me, though. One church where I was invited to speak took the meeting over because they didn't like my demonstration of joy, which to them just looked like silliness, I guess. Nonetheless, God hit me with even *more* joy that night. Believe me, I wasn't trying to presumptuously stir it up. Yes, I was hurt by their disapproval of my joy expression, but God stood beside me and said, "I'm giving it to you anyway . . . and a greater dose!" He taught me a lot during that time. I had to settle in my heart that His affirmation was more than enough for me. That's where true joy comes anyway. Challenges will come your way, fear may rear its ugly head, and trials are sure to be there. But if you know He is happy with you, you will have joy. It's joy that keeps you strong through it all—however difficult—to endure right on out to the other end.

Keep upgrading your joy level

I want to get back to the story of the season of trials. I kept the joy up day in, and day out. I was not only learning another level of joy warfare, I was learning to be vigilant with it. I started sending out those joy videos to this person and that person. I invited friends to come over and drink some Holy Ghost-joy with me. As we gathered together, we laughed a lot until we felt the Spirit take over. Then with all that joy bubbling over, I intentionally went after the lies that caused me to feel hopeless in the midst of the season of trials.

The result was that God rewarded me. The joy videos I sent out hit the mark and sparked several large church revival centers. They reignited and revitalized a lot of people. God was giving me a little reward for walking faithfully through those tough trials. You have to keep in mind that a trial doesn't last forever. After awhile, it has to let up. And it lets up when we have upgraded our joy-level and resolved in our hearts that His goodness is always toward us. If we fail to mature in our joy level, however, then the same trial will revisit us again and again . . . until we get it. I don't want that. I want to learn my lesson the first time!

I love what Peter says:

> *Dear friends, do not be surprised at the fiery ordeal that has come on you to test you, as though something strange were happening to you. But rejoice inasmuch as you participate in the sufferings of Christ, so that you may be* ***overjoyed*** *when his glory is revealed. If you are insulted because of the name of Christ, you are* ***blessed****, for the Spirit of* ***glory*** *and of God rests on you.*
>
> 1 Peter 4:12-14, emphasis added

The Blessed are Happy

If you are going through a trial, it should only be because you are blessed. By the way, "blessed" can also mean "happy,"[9] and is one of the definitions of a person who is "blessed" in the New Covenant. Being happy is a sign that the spirit of glory and Christ is on you. Glory is directly connected to God's goodness,[10] and His goodness is seen only by those with a thankful heart, which is a foundation of joy.

One of the other foundations of joy is *halal*,[11] the Hebrew word for "praise". Anyone can praise the Lord casually, but *halal*-praise is the high praise that will cause the seat of God's throne to be established in your midst. When you are full of joy, God enthrones Himself upon your praise. There's no better place in the middle of an intense trial than to be joyfully positioned before His throne.

The point is that as a happy prophet, live as one who is overflowing with joy—at the "overjoyed" level—with a lifestyle of rejoicing! You will be seen as a joy-filled, blessed-out, blissful, happy prophet. Sometimes the enemy gets ticked off because you are so happy and he starts to come at you. So what should you do? You need to take your joy to another level by physically moving yourself to a place of being *overjoyed*. You have to get heated up with so much joy that the enemy just can't take it any longer.

Joy takes the enemy out completely.

So get your joy on.

---

9 Strong's Greek Lexicon, #G3107, "*makarios*".
10 See Exod 33:18-19, NKJV.
11 Strong's Hebrew Concordance, #H1984, "*halal*".

Radically
Foolish
Joy-Prophets

Eight

I love going bonkers for Jesus. It's similar to going crazy over your favorite sports team winning their final and most prestigious game. Going all-out bonkers for Jesus is the kind of praise New Covenant prophets should have in their arsenal.

We prophets are the joyful heralds announcing the coming of God's Kingdom. The ministry of the prophet John the Baptist ushered in the physical presence of Jesus. In like manner, prophetic carriers of the New Covenant are called to usher in the presence of Jesus and His Kingdom on the earth but with upgraded weapons. Just as John the Baptist looked like a fool dressed in an odd style of clothing, we, too, may look a bit foolish to the casual bystander dressed uncommonly in the joy-atmosphere of Heaven.

Deploying the Joy Weapon

David is an Old Covenant example of this New Covenant action. He feigned insanity in the presence of his enemy and so escaped his grasp.

> *So he changed his behavior before them,*
> *pretended madness in their hands, scratched*

*on the doors of the gate, and let his saliva
fall down on his beard.*

1 Samuel 21:13

The Hebrew word for "madness" is the same word
from where we get "hallelujah", or *halal*, which translates
as "praise." It's fuller meaning, however, means, "to be
clamorously foolish"; "to boast"; "to celebrate"; "to rave";
"to act a madman"; in short, to go radically bonkers and
be stark raving mad in worship! When the enemy comes
at us, it is only the "foolish" praise of demonstrative,
uninhibited love expressions for our King that causes
him to let us go. Unreserved and wildly exaggerated
praise declared unashamedly in public is a tool every
New Covenant prophet should wield. One of my favorite
passages of *halal*-praise that I have used many times as a
part of this strategy in my life is found in 2 Chronicles 20:

*After consulting the people, Jehoshaphat
appointed men to sing to the LORD and to
praise him for the splendor of his holiness
as they went out at the head of the army,
saying:*

*"Give thanks to the LORD, for his love endures
forever."*

*As they began to sing and praise, the LORD
set ambushes against the men of Ammon
and Moab and Mount Seir who were invading
Judah, and they were defeated.*

vs 21-22

The prophets were the ones who gave the orders to
praise *halal*-style. King Jehoshaphat was the one who

enforced this command, and the people responded in radical praise, ensuring their victory. The lesson is this: When your enemies come to kill you, the best strategy is to just go crazy for Jesus.

I love *halal*-praise. It smacks in the face of religiosity and exposes any residual of dignity when you go bonkers and lift up wild praise for the King. Listen, when the enemy is advancing with evil intentions to destroy you, this New Covenant tool is a must to halt his assaults. We are not employing physical implements of warfare to deal with our enemy. Instead, we have access to the undefeatable power tools of Heaven guaranteeing our success: undignified and lavish praise.

I love the fact that *halal*-praise released such a breakthrough for the people of Israel; it took them three days to gather in the spoils of war after the enemy was thrown into utter confusion and turned on each other. That's the power of our *halal*-praise on the battlefront![12]

The New Covenant apostle and prophet, Paul and Silas, knew this tool well. After being arrested and thrown in jail for preaching the gospel, they started singing hymns and were praising God late into the night. They counted it a great privilege to suffer for His name, which was evident by their joyous and boisterous praise so that all the other prisoners could hear them singing. Suddenly, right in the midst of their uproarious praise-party, the Lord released a great earthquake where the prison broke apart and the prisoner's chains fell right off! Salvations were the results of that breakthrough.

Joyful praise is a strategic weapon of war for which New Covenant prophets are to be known. Many times I have been in a fearful state of depression, a "closed heaven", if you will. It is then that I have to get my radical

---

[12]   See 2 Chron 20:21-26.

praise on for the King. I look directly at Him in the Spirit and begin to worship, with an eye-to-eye focus upon Him alone. I dance, I shout, I praise, I run around the house, I leap, I sing—I go bonkers!—until breakthrough comes. Sometimes I do that in the streets too, because I don't care where I'm at when I praise Him. I belong to Jesus, and He deserves my unreserved worship. When I do that, He sees it, and He blesses me for it. He loves it when we give Him a sacrifice of praise from that place where it really costs us something, and any shred of pride will be revealed in the midst of our painful and difficult situation.

Is your picture of a prophet one who goes crazy in radical joyful worship to Jesus? Probably not. We normally think of a prophet as one who is very serious—an intense, humorless person. That must change . . . really. We are prophets of the *New* Covenant, not the Old. It's time we act like it.

"Tehilah"—God's Throne

Jesus Himself lives in the midst of the praises of His people. When we praise Him *halal*-style, something significant happens:

> But thou art holy, O thou that inhabitest the praises of Israel.

> Psalm 22:3, KJV

God's throne is not made of earthly matter, such as wood, gold, or silver; it is formed out of the praises of His people. Praise is what He inhabits—He lives there! The Hebrew word for "praise" used in this verse is *tehilah*[13],

---

[13] Strong's Hebrew Concordance, #H8416, *"tehilah"*.

which has at its roots the word, *halal*. God is enthroned upon the radical, crazy praise His sons and daughters release.

Praise Makes the Exchange

It is impossible for a spirit of heaviness to linger as you commit to praise Him. Isaiah 61 details what God gives us in exchange:

> *The oil of gladness instead of mourning, and a garment of praise instead of a spirit of despair.*

> v 3

Here we see the same word (*tehilah*) used where God removes heaviness as we offer up to Him radical praise. "Gladness" is the oil of joy that dispels mourning. Revelation 21 says:

> *"He will wipe every tear from their eyes."*

> v 4

God has no intention of allowing us to have anything other than a *glad* heart—a heart that is happy and full of joy—where there is no more sadness, depression, or heaviness. That's why part of our job as New Covenant radically foolish prophets is to fully possess a glad heart, offer Him continual foolish praise, and release Heaven's oil of joy wherever we are. Through these weapons of radical, bonkers, raving-mad *halal*-praise, we release all that is needed to those around us that will banish heaviness, bring healing to all who are mourning, and displace it with joy.

Joyful Praise Displaces Fear

Nine

Most prophets seem to have a major battle with fear at some point in his or her life. But every prophet must be free of fear if they are to fulfill the assignment the Lord has given them. Therefore, moving through fear is key to walking in a victorious ministry. I have discovered a type of praise that will break off all fear, which I want to explore here.

Kim Clement, an amazing prophet who died recently, was once asked how he was able to release the kind of words that impacted leaders of nations. He said:

> When I got free of fear, then God was able to entrust me with the kind of prophecies that impacted people deeply.

For a prophet, fear is a terrible enemy. Just like kryptonite shuts down Superman, so fear shuts down the prophet.

Fear manifests itself in many different ways. Sometimes fear masks itself as dignity and this was something I had to learn to identify and deal with.

Moving to Vacaville brought me into a place of feeling like I was walking with the big guys. Up to that time, I had been a wild prophetic man in the small town of Willits. But coming to Vacaville, I felt the need to be more dignified and ceremonious in my ways. I got to sit on the front row with the respected leadership team I had admired for so long. Little by little this need to *appear* like someone *important* was stealing the fresh release of power I needed in order to continue making an impact at God's leading.

The Undignified Fool's Dance

One day as I was walking the streets of Vacaville, God said to me, "Keith, you have gotten way too dignified . . . you need to do the fool's dance."

I thought, "Good one, Lord! Yes, I agree . . . maybe in a month or so. I'll get some guys and we'll do it together."

He said, "No . . . you need to do the dance now."

I was very familiar with the fool's dance. I did that on the seven-day joy-walk through those seven cities near my old hometown of Willits that I mentioned earlier. The heavens had actually opened on that joy-walk where I saw the Father standing and heard Him cheering me on, "There's My boy! I'm so proud of you, son."

I knew exactly what God was asking of me. I realized in that moment that I was stuck back in a place of fear. But this time, it had snuck up on me a different way . . . in the form of dignity. You know you are dealing with a spirit of fear when you don't know the people around you but you still are afraid to do a little public dance-jig of praise for the Lord.

Well, God called me on my fear-issue that day and had me get my dance on right there in the streets of Vacaville.

Now I didn't jump into a big dance because I was dealing with fear. I just sort of eased into it. Looking around, I casually slipped on my dark sunglasses, put my ear buds in and blasted the music, and then flipped up my hoodie, cinching the strings real tight so it covered a good portion of my face. Even still, I felt the fear. *What will people think of me?* Reluctantly, I started walking down the street. At first I swayed a bit from side-to-side, moving my feet hesitantly in a dance-like motion, nervously glancing about to see who might be driving by. But as I continued to jig-jog down the street, joy began to bubble up and take me over so that before I knew it, I was shouting and leaping and praising God wildly—full-on *halal*-style.

That is, until I ran into my neighbor.

Drat. One of the few guys I would actually know on the streets of Vacaville was now standing right in front of me with his Giants baseball cap on. He looked at me really puzzled and asked, "Keith? . . . Hey! What . . . what are you doing?"

When I finally gained a bit of composure from twirling wildly around for a mile or so and could see clearly who it was speaking to me, I mumbled out of breath, "Oh . . . a joy-thing!"

He surprised me then by asking, "Hey Keith! Where am I?" Even though we weren't that far from both of our houses—a place he had lived for fifteen years!—he seemed really confused as to where he was.

I now saw the prophetic picture starting to unfold. He had a Giants hat on. This "giant" I was dealing with in my life was dignity. When I began to praise God, the enemy (not my neighbor, of course) was brought into confusion. He was just manifesting the spiritual reality of what was happening in the atmosphere—confusion. But its greater purpose for why God wanted me to do the "dance" began to be revealed.

My neighbor asked me, "Can I walk with you the rest of the way home?"

"Sure!" I said, and we walked on together, talking about joy amongst other things.

That was a real breakthrough for me.

"Crazy" Acts of a Prophet

Sometimes prophets are required to do crazy things if they are going to be God's fool, one who can be entrusted with the King's message.

> *Then Jehu came out to the servants of his master, and one said to him, "Is all well? Why did this madman come to you?"*
>
> Kings 9:11, NKJV

This "madman" was the nameless prophet who had just poured a flask of oil on his head and anointed him as King of Israel with the command of Heaven to take out Ahab's house and Jezebel. Sometimes we have to settle it in our hearts that we are God's fools; we are a "jester" for the King. We are meant to please Him and Him alone.

Keep Your Praise On

You know the enemy likes to shut down the thanks and praise to the Lord that prophet's carry. The prophet Daniel was a man of integrity in every area. The enemy knew that, and so those who were jealous of his position in the King's administration tried to figure out a way to take him down.

> *Finally these men said, "We will never find*

any basis for charges against this man Daniel unless it has something to do with the law of his God."

Daniel 6:5

Their best idea was to find some way to take legal action against his fixed devotion to the Lord. Notice that this did not deter the prophet Daniel in the least.

Now when Daniel learned that the decree had been published, he went home to his upstairs room where the windows opened toward Jerusalem. Three times a day he got down on his knees and prayed, giving thanks to his God, just as he had done before.

v 10

The Lord will always reward public praise. This is sometimes required for prophets who want to go the distance, because at times, we are too concerned about what others think about our devotion to God. You see, the enemy doesn't care if you have a little fiery devotion. He just wants you to keep that fire in the fireplace. He doesn't mind if you have a little praise; just keep it in your private prayer closet. There is a time for private prayer, but there is also a time for public prayer that is observed by all. Which time is it for you at this present time? When you release praise *halal*-style with thanks, it sends a ripple effect into the enemy's camp. Praise of man and praise of God cannot reside in the same place. Praise of man is actually called the fear of man—something completely unacceptable for His prophets.

Of course, we know how the story ended with Daniel. He maintained his steadfast devotion to God, trusted

Him, and all his enemies perished. Daniel's faithfulness and complete trust in the Lord resulted in a promotion in the King's service and greater prosperity than before.

> *So Daniel prospered during the reign of Darius and the reign of Cyrus the Persian.*

v 28

When you confront fear head-on with praise—especially a public display of praise—it may not lead directly to promotion, it may first lead to the lion's den. But just know that the Lord watches out for those who are His and He delivers them out of fear's trap.

Humility breaks the dignity spirit

I had a pastor come up to me one day and ask me to pray for him. He said he was struggling with fear and that God had told him to have me pray for him. I asked the Lord what He wanted me to tell the man. The Lord told me very quickly that He wanted the man to do the fool's dance. I knew what that meant, for I had just done my fool's dance to break the dignity-spirit.

So I delivered God's message to the pastor: "Go to the place where you care the most about what people think of you. Then dance and praise God like crazy, and you will be free of fear."

He stared at me for a moment, and then looked down as he walked away, clearly disappointed and looking dejected. It reminded me of the moment when Naaman wanted Elisha to personally pray for him. He thought he could just get the prophet's hand waved over his body with a power prayer released over him and he'd be completely healed. But instead, Elisha told him to go dunk himself seven times in the dirty Jordan River. Such an act was humiliating to a man of his prestigious position in the Syrian army. But it was just what the "doctor" ordered. Miracles require humility, and God knew Naaman needed a measure of that. When he finally did decide to humble himself by dipping in the Jordan River as instructed by the prophet, he was completely healed, and a brand new clean man emerged, both physically and spiritually. Returning home to Syria, he was transformed inside and out and became a follower of Jehovah.

I believe if the pastor who asked me to pray for him took the word God gave him and humbled himself, he too would have received all his heart desired.

No one should determine the measure of your praise

Praise is an amazing and powerful weapon that all prophets must have under their belt. There is no dignified praise allowed when you are serving the King of kings. A pastor friend of mine was once told to quiet down his radical praise for which he was known. Prior to becoming a believer, this same pastor had spent several years in prison for a drunk-driving incident where a young friend was killed. Amazingly, the family of the one killed released their forgiveness to him, and he was subsequently led to the Lord.

When this pastor was asked to quiet down his praise, he replied, "You didn't get me out of prison, release mercy to me or set me free, so you don't get to determine the measure of my praise."

This is the proper response to releasing our praise unashamedly to God! No one is able to stop our praise or determine its level. This pastor recognized the grace of God in his life and he wasn't about to level off his thanks to the Lord for delivering his soul from its torment and imprisonment.

If the enemy can't steal your voice, he'll try to steal the passion and intensity of how you worship. Praise and worship is fuel to the prophetic word. If you want to stand in front of kings and release the word of the Lord, you must first learn how to be a friend with the King of kings. When you are His friend, you will have access to the kings of this earth who need to hear from the King of the universe, and God will set up prearrangements for you. You will be His spokesperson and an ambassador to the nations where He sends you. And that should be enough to fill you with joyful praise in the face of any fear.

The King First

Ten

One day in prayer, the Lord began to give me a prophetic word about an influencer I was to meet in another country. He gave me a few vague clues I was supposed to search for to find this person, and then He gave me a prophetic word for the country of that specific leader. Little did I know how it was all going to come about.

Before I get into this story let me say that sometimes students ask me for an impartation of my prophetic gift or of the power that I carry. They often don't understand that the gift didn't actually start with the gift itself; it started with an *encounter* with the King of kings. People want to impact kings, but they haven't yet learned how to be intimate with *the* King. I didn't seek after prophecy. I sought after the King—always putting Him first—and He began to lead me into a prophetic journey through intimacy with Him. Now I am not saying I don't passionately pursue the prophetic gift, neither am I downplaying the hunger and pursuit of the gifts of the Holy Spirit. I just know the source of those gifts is God Himself. You get the Giver and the gifts will follow. You pursue the gifts apart from intimate friendship with the Giver, and one day He could deny ever knowing you."

> *Many will say to me on that day, "Lord, Lord, did we not prophesy in your name, and in*

your name drive out demons and in your name perform many miracles?" Then I will tell them plainly, "I never knew you. Away from me, you evildoers!"

Matthew 7:22-23

That Greek word for "knew" is *ginosko[14]*, which refers to the intimacy a healthy husband and wife share together. In other words, you can do ministry and still miss encountering God in an intimate way that draws Him close to you. Now I want the gifts, but the Giver has captured me. In His presence is the totality of all my joy. When I get caught up in His love for me, and my love for Him, then radical, joy-filled boldness follows.

So let's get back to the story of getting a word for an influencer. This whole incident came from that place of intimacy. As I was just hanging out with Jesus one day, He showed me a prophetic word for someone I would meet in another country I was about to travel to in a few weeks.

After I arrived and ministered in that nation for several days, I was pressed by the Spirit to go out on a walk one day, not knowing where I would end up. Sure enough I found one of the clues He had given me just a few weeks before. Then I found another clue. But I didn't know where to go from there. I had ended up on my walk in front of a fire station with a lot of workers outside. I stood there watching them finish up their duties and then head back inside the station.

I felt really strong that I needed to speak to those fire station workers and pondered what to do. Then I heard the Lord say, "You have to walk by faith."

---

[14]   Strong's Greek Lexicon, #G1097, *"ginosko"*, meaning "to know".

So I mustered up the courage I needed and headed inside the fire station. I didn't know what to do with the prophetic word or whom it was for, so I just gave the prophetic word to the men and women in uniform inside. They were gracious to receive that word, and politely informed me that it was not for any of them, but they gave me a number to call.

So I blessed them, left, and called the number, only to find out it was a national hotline that didn't seem to get me anywhere specific. Through several other seemingly disconnected events, I ended up meeting with a leader of that nation. I was able to give him the prophetic word, and as I did, more prophetic words bubbled out for him and his wife. That opened up yet another door where I ended up at their house prophesying over many other leaders as well.

When you walk by faith in obedience to what the Lord is showing you in those times of intimacy, He will promote you before the kings of the earth.

Strategy in Prophetic Ministry

Prophetic ministry started really taking off for me in that particular country and other nations as well. But God was quickly upgrading *how* I ministered in the prophetic.

For several years I had a particular challenge as I was growing in my prophetic ministry. I didn't know how to set personal boundaries that would allow me to refuse requests for prophetic ministry. I was afraid to tell people, "No . . . I can't." Part of the challenge is that our gift is validated as we prophesy over people. It can be very easy, then, to become a people-pleaser where we fear if we refuse to prophesy on demand, we won't be asked back to that place. We can become more concerned about what people think of us if we don't, than fearing if God is really leading us to prophesy. Having no established boundaries in our ministry sets us up for many temptations and problems as prophets, and is definitely a joy stealer. When you are unable to say "no" to people, you end up walking in the fear of man, which is a snare of the enemy. You will continue to minister, but you may eventually grow to despise the very ones to whom you minister. I must frequently remind myself that I am ultimately serving the King and people are not to be my master, but are rather, the recipients of healthy affection and kindness. Only when I am truly in close connection with the Lord is there sustainable joy. Outside of that I can quickly get into obligatory service just to please people as they make their demands on my gift.

As I began to grow in my prophetic ministry, more and more people wanted me to minister prophetically over them. Soon I found the grace to minister to long lines of people diminishing. It quickly become clear God was redirecting me. He began to teach me that I could prophesy over many people, but I needed to be strategic about who I was to prophesy over.

Operate as a king

I had a prophetic mentor tell me, "Keith, as you move forward with your prophetic gift you have to learn to operate as a king. You invite those individuals into connection with you for whom you have a strategic word. You don't just prophesy over everyone. You must be intentional." In that particular season, his word was right on. I felt the grace running out to prophesy over every person who approached me. It almost felt a bit like I was prostituting my gift. It wasn't their fault; I had not yet learned how to set healthy boundaries.

The result of this was that for a good year, my prophetic gift shut down—all because I could not say "no" to people. When you don't establish clear boundaries with your prophetic gift, your emotions will start manifesting a "no" until you learn to verbalize it. It was not a fun process. I would go to places I normally ministered and no prophetic word would come out. And yet, that is exactly why I had been invited—to release my prophetic gift.

I remember one place in particular where the Lord was trying to hone this new skill in me. The church had brought me in the year before and told me I was their new favorite speaker. Quickly I was going to become the opposite of their favorite. I attempted to tell the leaders who invited me that I couldn't operate in the previous fashion of prophesying over *everyone*, and that God was being more strategic with me. That didn't seem to go over well with this particular minister. He just grinned and patted me on the back, saying, "Oh, the prophetic will be there tomorrow, brother, when you need it."

Well, the next day came around and the prophetic wasn't there. I tried to bring it out, but nothing significant came. I felt bad, of course, but that was part of the problem. I didn't *need* to feel bad. God had given me a treasure, and He had specific assignments for that treasure.

Determine to follow the Spirit's lead

The evening meeting came and God hit me with the spirit of joy. I was so filled up before the service in the pastor's office that I became drunk in the Spirit. Intoxicated with joy, I stumbled out into the meeting where I was scheduled to speak and wound up prophesying over just about every person present. The grace was there that night to prophesy over anyone and everyone. I even ministered to one of the family members of the pastor who had a problem with God and the church. That night, her life was radically altered.

Unfortunately, even with the obvious fruit of my prophetic ministry that night, it didn't find its way into the pastor's heart. He was offended. Why? Because I didn't prophesy at the specified time he had allotted; instead, only a nice sermon came out. And the night that I was supposed to give a message, joy and prophecy flowed out. The pastor wasn't able to control it. He got nervous because he still had two meetings scheduled with me, so he called a senior prophet he knew to try to get some advice on how to handle me. The senior prophet said, "Just watch and see the fruit of the next meetings."

Well, the fruit was good . . . and God was also setting me free. I was learning that if I wanted to stay in a place of joy, I must respond to His Spirit and not perform on cue to others' demand on my gift. My challenge was to try to honor leaders the best I could in the situation, but not at the expense of grieving the Spirit of God and His leading.

Where there is fear of man, there is no true freedom. Sustainable joy is one of the fruits of freedom. If you desire the favor of God, you cannot live to please man; you must choose between the two. The King must always be your top priority as a prophet, and following His lead, despite pressure to the contrary, is the pathway to a sustainable and highly productive prophetic ministry. Keeping the King first in your life is the only way to ensure victory over the fear of man.

Sustainable Joy

Eleven

A couple years ago through a number of events the Lord identified a crack in my foundation. Now that is never good to hear. But I am so thankful when He shows me those things. Abundant life is always going to come on the other side of getting the problem fixed and implementing God's solution. As I've said before, traveling to nations often reveals areas in my life that are incompatible to the ways of the Kingdom. If I am going to impact a nation, the strongholds of that nation must not have any hold in me.

I was ministering in a foreign country for about ten days, a place I had never been before. As I came home following the trip, however, I went three weeks without sleep. That is torturous, because sleep deprivation affects the mind so that you feel like you're going crazy. Graciously, the Lord showed me through a dream of my wife's that I had picked up a curse through a trinket a little girl had given me on that trip. I broke the trinket, threw it out, the curse lifted, and my sleep was restored.

Crack in the Foundation

Soon after this, other things began to surface in my life from that trip that I needed to address. It was then that the Lord spoke to my spirit, "Keith, you have a crack in your foundation." I could tell something was bubbling up from the last few months that needed adjustment, but when He told me that, it sent me on an intentional quest to discover what it was.

I heard the Lord say to my spirit: "Just as the country you visited recently had ancestral worship as its stronghold, so too, you have spiritual ancestral worship as a stronghold in your own life." This particular nation worshiped their ancestors, and the Lord was showing me that like them, I had put my spiritual fathers on a pedestal—a place solely reserved for the King of the universe. For me, it manifested as another form of fear. Ouch. What a joy crusher that was.

As He began to unpack this revelation, I could see that I cared more about what my spiritual fathers thought of me than what the Lord thought of me. These fathers had actually become a mediator between God and me, and I knew He wanted His place rightfully restored. Whenever I was in a dilemma or needed advice, the first thing I did was contact one of my spiritual fathers. Now there is wisdom in seeking counsel, for sure. But for me personally, it was out of balance. God wanted me to learn to go to Him first with the expectation that I was going to hear from Him on the issue. Then, and only after I had spent time with Him, could I go and check in with a spiritual father to get a bit of a confirmation on what I believed God was telling me.

I realized I had elevated these spiritual fathers to a higher position than my heavenly Father. I immediately asked the Lord to quickly take them off that pedestal. When you have spiritual fathers in a place reserved for God alone, you cannot have true joy. You are always trying so hard to please the fathers, and when you feel that you aren't able to, it can be really distressing. Your emotions are up and down according to what you perceive your spiritual father's view is towards you. Within a couple weeks, God answered my prayer through an unexpected and embarrassing situation that exposed this elevated place of spiritual fathers on my foundation.

I had been in a discussion with some folks by email that had been going back and forth—one of these was a spiritual father. I was a bit frustrated with how things were being done and so I decided to vent through an email message, never intending to send it out, of course . . . I was just venting, expressing my thoughts and feelings as I typed. I had planned on rewriting it more appropriately in the morning. On and on I ranted, releasing all the pent-up frustrations I felt about that situation and the people involved, etc., and then to my bewilderment, the email just disappeared. It was so late that night and I was kind of stunned as I wondered where it went . . . *Oh well,* I thought as I stumbled off to bed. *I'll find it and fix it in the morning.*

The next morning my wife woke me up with an urgent, "How could you do that?"

Confused, and struggling to understand, I replied, "Do what?"

"You sent that email!" Right then I realized I had inadvertently clicked "send" to everyone on that particular list, including one of my spiritual fathers.

I knew, then, I was in for a shaking. God was answering my prayer and I was about to get free of putting spiritual fathers on a pedestal, because I had just ticked one off. I hit the sore spot in his heart in my venting, and not only him, but everyone else who read the email. My rantings did not put him—and a few others—in a good light, that's for sure.

Well, that caused a series of meetings to be set up and lots of damage control I had to walk through. I was pretty freaked out. My fear of man erupted. I thought, *For sure I have lost all favor with man and my prophetic days are over and done. . . .*

In the end, it wasn't as bad as I imagined, but it wasn't pretty either. The meetings were really intense as we worked through the issues.

New Tools to Live By

During those sessions with my leaders, I decided to put myself through a week-long intensive inner healing ministry called, "Restoring the Foundations," which ultimately was life-changing for me. It showed me where I had elevated spiritual fathers in my life in an unhealthy way. It gave me some great tools and new mindset beliefs, and exposed where the unhealthy ones originated.

It took a few months to learn how to walk out these new beliefs and see the inner healing begin to take effect in my life. It was clearly evident to people who knew me that the results of the healing brought a verifiable upgrade in my life. One of the beliefs I learned during those inner healing sessions was to readily extend mercy to people when they make mistakes. Just as I needed mercy, they did also. I had never been able to give spiritual fathers mercy and had never seen them in their humanity until then. I guess I was expecting them to be as infallible as God. I had always seen them as ones who didn't have the right to be wrong. So if they *did* do something wrong, I was totally offended. While these fathers had played a vital role in my development by revealing an attribute or two of who God is, they were *not* God. Though that may sound so obvious and simplistic, it was life-changing for me—the pivotal moment where I learned to truly honor my spiritual fathers and the Holy Spirit's anointing on them, while extending great mercy to their humanness.

Whenever I see myself starting to get bitter at someone, I then remember, "Oh yes! That person is only human." I step back and choose to extend much grace and mercy to them. It changes my whole attitude towards them immediately.

Healing brings joy

One of the things God gave me in exchange for bitterness was—you guessed it!—joy. Instead of responding bitterly to those who offended me, I quickly learned that extending mercy to people was what released natural joy. And joy keeps the heart happy, and honestly, being a happy prophet is a much-preferred way to live day to day.

Forgive from the heart

Forgiving people from the heart is a huge challenge for us all. It can be especially difficult for those within our closest circles with whom we have greater expectations, but so necessary. Prophets can be very black and white at times, so that when an injustice is done to them or they experience an unkind reaction as a response to their ministry, there is sometimes a desire to retaliate, no matter who it is. That was my thinking. I knew that I couldn't hold in an offense, so I would have to work through forgiving the person I felt had broken trust, or the one who had committed a wrongdoing towards me or someone I cared for. That had at least kept me in the game for some years, but God was going after a higher upgrade. What I really needed to do was to accept them in their humanity as ones who make mistakes and are *going* to make mistakes in the future.

People will make mistakes

It is important to accept that your leaders, your boss and co-workers, your spouse, your children, your parents, and your friends *will* make mistakes. It's okay. They're human. You'll live . . . they'll live . . . even after their mistakes. And so with this upgraded thinking, I, too, began to live.

I saw a picture from the Lord that helped me begin to turn this all around so I was not focused on offenses.

> *Deceit is in the hearts of those who plot evil,*
> *but those who promote peace have joy.*

> Proverbs 12:20

You see, I needed to learn to promote peace instead of stirring up strife, tension, disagreements, and being critical and unmerciful. How? He took me back to a memory of when I was young and spilled the milk at the dinner table. I would sometimes be sent to my bedroom when that happened, but only after being sternly chastised for my irresponsibility.

Food fight

Then God gave me a new picture of that scenario. It was me spilling the milk at the dinner table and the heavenly Father sitting across from me. I watched as He took some food off the table and playfully threw it at me announcing, "Food fight!" He didn't get angry with me. Instead, He jovially joined in the mess I had just made with the spilled milk and turned something that could have been an unmerciful moment of anger and punishment into something humorous and fun. How good He is.

Now whenever I start to get upset at someone for something they did, I sense God remind me, "Food fight,

Keith! Have some fun, and extend them some mercy. They're just human. Give 'em a break. See the good in them instead of headlining the error of their ways or highlighting how they wronged you or that person. Food fight!"

There is sustainable joy for those who promote peace in every situation. Those who continually stir up strife, however, will never find peace. Going after peaceful relationships gladdens the heart of the Father who is known as the Reconciler. Mercy and peace will always nurture greater joy.

The Foundation
of Joy

Twelve

Proverbs 12 lays out the foundation of joy for us:

There is joy for those that promote peace.

v 20

Clearly joy is only sustainable if something very healthy is established at a deeper level of a person's life: living as a peace-promoter. Have you ever seen someone who has a great time at a Holy Ghost party, but you know it is not sustainable? Why is that? They have strife at home, in their marriage, within their extended family, at work, or with their pastor. Conflicts and disharmony seems to mark their life as a whole. Only peace-promoters live in genuine joy and it is exhibited in their healthy and harmonious relationships. As prophets, that's what we are going for.

Live Peaceably

I learned a key early on in ministry. You can open the heavens through great worship, prophetic ministry, and stir up joy everywhere you go, but the heavens will only stay open where healthy relationships are intact. The Bible says that our struggle is not against flesh and blood[15], but that is exactly where the devil initiates the fight. He goes after the unhealed relational dysfunctions resident in our heart.

You see, joy is like the overflow of a violently surging stream as it gushes out and cascades down a mountaintop. Though rivers flow as a powerful force deep within a mountain, we often only see the trickle of water on the surface in comparison to what lies beneath. Peace is like that deep water current within a believer that causes joy to bubble up and flow out of their life easily. If you don't nurture peace in your relationships, genuine joy is inaccessible. But if it's there, it will burst out and even breach its banks.

In order for that to happen, however, prophets must learn how to cultivate peace in all their relationships until they are healed and healthy and living as peaceable as possible.

Trust is the Environment for Peace

But even deeper than peace is trust. You can't have sustainable peace if you haven't learned to trust. You can try to release the word of the Lord all you want, but if you haven't built trust, at the end of the day you are not going to advance the Kingdom. Trust creates an environment for peace.

> *Trust in the LORD with all your heart, and lean not on your own understanding; in all your ways acknowledge Him, and he shall direct your paths.*

> Proverbs 3:5-6, NKJV

---

[15]   See Eph 6:12.

It's impossible to trust if you are always trying to figure everything out. Prophets oftentimes want to know everything that is going on. They think they see everything, but in truth, they only see in part. They must learn to trust when they can't see beyond their understanding in order to progress into maturity.

I remember years ago when God gave me Kris Vallotton as a mentor. Unknowingly, I made it hard for him the first five years of our mentorship. Why? I didn't trust. I thought to myself, *What does he know? I know as much as him, and anyway, I know his strengths and weaknesses.* I wouldn't say that out loud, of course, but deep down, those were my thoughts. There came a point when Kris finally said to me, "Maybe you should find a different mentor, Keith . . . one that you can trust. I don't feel like I'm getting through to you." He went on to say that he didn't like to see me hurting so much. He could tell I was resisting him every step of the way. You can't make progress when you're resisting. It was then that I talked to the Lord and He confirmed what Kris had told me: I did not know how to trust. The Lord went on to say, "I have given you Kris to help nurture and develop you."

Determine to Trust Others

In that moment I decided to trust. Shortly after that decision, I had an issue that needed addressing, so I called Kris. He recommended what to do to resolve the issue. My first thoughts were, *That can't be right!* But then I remembered I had made a vow to the Lord to trust. So I took a leap of faith and chose to trust Kris' word. I did what he said without arguing or questioning. As soon as I did that, I saw how right the decision was. My eyes were opened, and I suddenly realized that Kris was indeed seeing at a much higher level than I was. *He really* was *trying to help me.* After that, something changed in me that altered the next five years of our mentorship. From then on it was like friends just hanging out—easy, light, and without the tension of resistance from my end.

Prophets must learn to trust, because that is where joy is found. When you are always anxious about everything, feeling the weight of the world on your shoulders, so to speak, it's very difficult to trust. But as you do, you'll find peace in it, and peace is the mountain from where joy flows.

The Greater Reality of "I am loved"

Learning to trust people is really vital. Trusting in someone bigger than you is a must. But in order for that to happen you have to be convinced that you are really and truly loved by them. *How can you trust someone if you're not sure they really love you?*

That is one of the biggest challenges for prophets—learning to be loved. Elijah felt he had no one who loved him. Samson had a problem with finding healthy love. Moses felt at times everyone was against him. Prophets often deal with rejection issues because they feel the word they are carrying is being rejected. At such times they may feel that people don't love them because they aren't receiving them, but they don't know why. They don't understand why people won't readily accept their word or the powerful heavenly concept they've shared. They *know* it is a good one. *It's from God, after all, isn't it?* So they deal with rejection again and again.

Until one day, they begin to live from a higher reality: "I am loved." What a great truth for prophets to live by.

Love is Greater, Love will Endure

For prophets to choose love over what is right and wrong is actually a huge win. It ensures healthy relationships all around. Prophets will often be willing to give up all for the word of the Lord rather than choosing to love. But love is greater than proving that the word of the Lord is right. Now while I agree that the word of the Lord is absolutely important, love is greater. Scripture says prophecies will disappear[16], but love will remain[17]. Choosing instead to love the ones to whom the word is intended and allowing yourself to be loved by others is a huge breakthrough for prophets.

Sometimes I have to choose to love my children even if they have not walked out clear instructions that were given to them. They chose to disobey, and yes, their disobedience has a consequence. But for me to choose to love them and extend mercy is always best. Sometimes prophetic people can get so caught up in the fact that people broke a rule or they didn't follow through with their word or they responded indifferently or refused to implement the word of the Lord. But prophets must learn that love *always* wins.

Love apart from God is counterfeit. Love isn't just a verb; it's a Person and it is only found in the Father's love.

> *God so loved the world that he sent his only begotten son.*
>
> John 3:16

Jesus is God's loving embrace, direct from the Father.

---

[16] See 1 Cor 13:8.

[17] ibid.

Isn't that how the Father is towards us? He is so patient. His is the only enduring love. When we fall short, He still loves us. If we never get free, He still loves us. Even though our own disobedience, sin, and offensive thoughts are destructive and are hurting us, He still loves us. He is wooing and drawing us back by speaking gently as He urges us, "Come to Me." That is where we, as prophets, can finally learn to let go and be gracious to others, because of His tenderness to us. His generous grace will cause us to act in the same manner.

To sum up, the following are keys for sustainable love, joy, and peace, and trusting others.

- Sustainable joy is found residing in an environment of peace.

- Peace is only sustainable as you trust someone greater than yourself.

- Trusting someone is only sustainable if you know that the person you are trusting really and truly loves you.

- The Father is the one who loved you so much, He sent Jesus for you. That is where sustainable joy comes from—a good and loving Father.

- Enduring love is only found in the heavenly Father's loving embrace.

His Love is Patient

I came into this renewal move of God in the late 90s kicking and screaming. I was a resister. Yet, God saw my heart crying out for more and He brought me into the more. The "more" was His tangible love. He captured me even when I was against what He was doing. I was like Saul of Tarsus, in a way, bent on persecuting the expression of the Church that was exploding in great joy on the earth at that time in renewal, in the prophetic, with inner healing, and the demonstration of the Father's love. I had gotten tripped up with the expressions of the outpouring of His Spirit. *This can't be God!* I said. Why? It didn't fit my religious grid for how God did things. But He was so patient with me and captured me with His love anyway. He brought spiritual fathers and mothers alongside of me who helped unveil the unconditional love of the Father. Then the Lord began to personally visit me with His extravagant love and I was ruined.

Whenever I start to get upset and judgmental at someone who is bound by religious traditions, and they may even be coming against me personally in some way, the Father then reminds me of His own patience with me. "Look at how I have loved you, son. The love I extended to you won over your heart."

It's then that I recall again how He wooed my heart with His patient love, and I know that I, too, must demonstrate that same patience. That is a good exercise for a prophet: remember how patient He was with your own past mistakes. It reminds me of when Peter denied the Lord three times. And yet, shortly after that incident, God, in His merciful grace completely restored Peter and gave him great authority to lead the Church into a new day. He didn't demand a big timeout for Peter. Instead, he reinstated him, and even gave him a big promotion—all of this shortly after his greatest fall! It is good for us to remember our own tendencies and shortcomings in order that we can be gracious with others' weaknesses, sins, and tendencies to stray.

When we don't forgive or we choose not to walk in grace towards others, we find our hearts have cooled and our love has diminished to little or nothing. Sometimes we begin to fill the void with false comforters or counterfeit joy-generators, when the bigger reality is, we just need to yield to a good Father and allow His love to fill us to overflowing again.

When love is our first choice and has been given an environment to thrive, our foundation of joy is always secure.

An Ecstatically Fun Holy Spirit

Thirteen

A minister once told me that the picture the Lord showed him of the Holy Spirit was seen in the Shroud of Turin, the burial cloth that supposedly covered Jesus' body when He was laid in the grave. Purportedly, it still retains the facial features of a person (believed to be Jesus' face) bearing a very grave expression. This pastor said that when he envisions the Holy Spirit, he looks like that—mournfully somber and easily grieved.

Yes, the Holy Spirit can be grieved at times, as we all can. We can be disheartened or saddened by people's inability to respond appropriately to our love or the Father's love. The same is true of the Holy Spirit. But I believe Him to be a much more fun-loving, joyful representation of God the Father rather than the Shroud of Turin depiction.

Representing Him

Our job as prophets is to bring the Holy Spirit's true presence into the earth. Prophets love and live for the presence of God. They are often representations of what the Holy Spirit is doing. When we carry around the word of God in us that we are birthing in the earth, we tend to get too serious about the time it takes for that word to be fulfilled.

For instance, not long ago I was in a focused time of praying and going after revival in the great State of California. But I was getting rather frustrated during one evening meeting I was leading, deeply pained by those who had not yet stepped into the word I was carrying with the same degree of passion. I was sensing an urgent timeframe but not seeing the same response. As I looked back at how I communicated the word that night, I realized that I had allowed some anger out of personal grief to seep through my prophetic release. That is never a good representation of the Holy Spirit. God is good, and He still follows through wonderfully despite our shortcomings. But as we speak on His behalf and in His name, we have to work on representing Him well in every situation.

Like I've said before, I've seen the Holy Spirit laughing at me sometimes. Not in derision, of course, but in wanting me to enjoy myself more. In doing so, He will often lovingly reveal secrets to me that help me overcome the enemy by defusing his plan. He is so gracious to me.

Here's an important key: prophets reflect the God they see. If we see the Holy Spirit as the easily-grieved One, we, too, will reflect that. With such a view of God, we will be very tense people to be around. In the process of communicating His word, we can also be very intense. While prophets are passionate to see what God has revealed to them come forth—as they should be!—they often must learn that the Holy Spirit is very, very patient in the process, not wanting any to perish. This alone should temper us, especially in the waiting.

His Wild Side

But what if our picture of God was focused more on His playful, ecstatically wild side? The Holy Spirit is literally the Spirit of Jesus on the earth. So what you see in the life of Jesus, you know the Holy Spirit carries, too. I've heard it said many times that the Holy Spirit is a perfect gentleman, and yet, I've witnessed Him to be rather wild at times, releasing ecstatic joy in seemingly all the wrong places. I've seen people so mad at the Holy Spirit as He is manifesting His wild side, yet He is the one who hovered over the earth at the very beginning of creation! This earth belongs solely to Him, and He doesn't want to be a stranger. As God, the Holy Spirit should be allowed every right to manifest however He desires in our midst.

Sometimes people have a hard time with my ecstatic side. You see, I received a manifestation of the Holy Spirit in my late twenties after I had been learning about joy for several years in the midst of accusation. As I said earlier, it wasn't an easy two-year process, but the Lord had promised that when I learned joy, He would remove the accusation and increase the anointing. Sure enough He did, and He did it in front of hundreds of ministers that were not familiar or necessarily welcoming of that type of manifestation. He's pretty funny sometimes.

He doesn't seem to mind messing up people's ideas of how things should be. I think He's rather bored with most of our meetings and intentionally walks in to mess up our slick plans and well-coiffed hair, so to speak. We can be way too predictable, but He is so creative and wants to have fun! I love allowing the ecstatic side of God in me to emerge whenever and wherever *He* desires. I decided a long time ago that I am not going to be in charge of determining when the Holy Spirit can be turned on and off in my life.

I was ministering at a revival that had been going on for over a year. It was my first time there, and even though it was termed a "revival", I made up my mind to have a great night. Sometimes we think we know what that looks like, but when we yield to the Holy Spirit, He may have something else in mind.

We are a reflection of the picture of God we have. Do you like the picture you're portraying?

That night, and to my surprise, I started off my preaching time with a heavenly tongue in what seemed like Arabic. I hadn't experienced that kind of tongue before and it certainly wasn't preplanned. It was passionate and certain with a determined flow that could not be stopped. I knew the people were wondering what in the world was going on since it was not normal protocol to begin preaching by speaking in tongues in such a way. But I also knew that if I were to stop and explain to them what I was doing, I'd be quenching the Spirit. It was very clear to me that I was speaking under a true inspiration of His Spirit that would have a definitive result. There are times when we can do things decently and in order, and at other times, the Holy Spirit decides that something a bit out of the norm is decently and in order. He is God, we are not.

Well, this night was one of those nights. This tongue seemed to go on and on and on. I kept thinking to myself as I was walking up and down the platform with the microphone speaking in this Arabic tongue: *Keith! You should be doing something! You're the guest speaker. Introduce yourself, at least! Say something . . . in English!*

I mean, I like moving in the Holy Spirit and all, but on this night, even *I* was a bit uncomfortable. The Holy Spirit didn't seem to mind one bit. After a long ten minutes of this, I found myself still going strong in that tongue with no sign of a let up. Just then, I watched a woman walk up to the front row of the congregation and lean down to speak to the pastor who was overseeing the meeting. He then walked over and asked me for the microphone.

"Guys, Keith has been speaking in an Arabic dialect that these two ladies right here understand." He went on to explain what the ladies heard me speaking in their language. Well, the place immediately exploded with praise to God and ministry flowed effortlessly with freedom the rest of the evening.

The ecstatic nature of the Spirit of God is so fun, but at times, it tests me and all those around me. I didn't pick to be this way; He chose me. The Holy Spirit sometimes likes to have a wild time. I think His purpose is to intentionally move outside of our boxed-in program. Many times when I am ministering in an ecstatic joy with my head shaking wildly as I'm jumping up and down and bouncing around the room in outbursts of high praise, it is because I'm sensing God's breakthrough is about to bust through the narrow and rigid confines to where we've relegated Him. People get so stuck sometimes in an inferior atmosphere. I hear people talk about a meeting sometimes like it was the high end of the presence of God. But I know there is so much more way higher, and whenever I get a chance, I help facilitate and yield to the Holy Spirit's release to that end.

And yet, I want *more* . . . and *even more* . . .

His Fool

Like I said before, sometimes you have to be a fool for the King if you want the King to show up. We like to talk about the King, but if we truly want Him present in our midst, then He is the only one who gets to remain in charge. We, on the other hand, must humble ourselves and be willing to look like fools if we truly want His presence.

I believe there is a greater move of God coming on this earth, but it is coming to those who are fully yielded to

Him in every way. I take serious this quote:

> *I set myself on fire and people come to watch me burn.*

I know that when I feel God wants to do something in a room, I actually have to become what He is doing. If I am going to be speaking on revival, I have to be revived. If I am going to speak on joy, I have to carry joy. If I am going to speak on love, I have to carry love towards the very ones I speak to. **A message is more caught than taught.** When I get consumed with the Holy Spirit's message and don't care what people think or say, then and only then will God show up. I may look like a fool but I am being very intentional to honor the Holy Spirit.

The Authentic Me

Bob Jones said that sometimes people wanted his prophetic gift, but they didn't want Bob Jones, the prophet, to come minister. I have had that happen a few times, too. People would ask me to come minister, but then specify what portions of my ministry (of me) they wanted. I have to communicate to them (in an honoring manner, of course) that I must always be the authentic person God made me—all portions of me. Then I often add, "Perhaps I'm not the right person you need to invite."

I have tried for too long to fit into the varying demands and specific criteria asked of me just to please the leaders. "Keith, we really need you to minister in this way . . . but please, not *that* way." I've found that when I comply to their demands, I wind up shutting down the Holy Spirit— the very one ministering through me. To please those people where I was invited, I have, a time or two, chosen not to minister in the Holy Spirit in the way I know best pleases Him. I won't ever do that again.

I have been speaking a long time and know how to honor protocol, but I have also learned that honoring the Lord is the preferred protocol. Sometimes a leader or pastor will want me to minister on joy. I remember during a particular conference, I could see in the spirit the whole region lacked healthy relationships. I felt the Holy Spirit shining His light on that issue. I did my best to honor what the leader needed at that conference without grieving the Holy Spirit. Where they had been hoping I would release an atmosphere of laughter and joy, instead I felt pressed to speak about the key to sustainable joy is having healthy relationships. Boom. I honored both the leader's desire for the conference theme *and* the Holy Spirit's. That's a win-win in my book. God knows how to set things up best.

Sometimes people want the joy of the Lord to enter the room but only *after* I have been ministering on joy. Sometimes it happens that way, sometimes it doesn't. After I've given it all I've got in my joy-message, I think to myself, *Hopefully laughter is going to break out now in the place.* But instead, tears and crying erupt! Seeing this unexpected response, I know the Lord is up to something so I ask Him, *What are You doing?* I have come to learn that sometimes He needs to first heal the deep wounds in the hearts of the people that have *stolen* their joy. So their response to my message and to God's presence may look different than my own preconceived ideas. Maybe I don't get the big laughter-and-joy meeting I want. But later on, the healed hearts learn how to live a *lifestyle* of joy, so much more preferred than if they would have been coerced into a hyped-up joy expression in that meeting.

Effectively partnering with the Holy Spirit *wherever* and *however* He so desires, in all situations and according to His plan, is really rewarding and fun, and is the place where His enthusiastic joy is released.

A Joy-Filled Life

Fourteen

Some people can enjoy the Holy Spirit in a meeting but they do not know how to live a life of *enjoyment*. If you are to go the distance as a healthy and happy New Covenant prophet, you have to learn the rhythm of a joyful life. How is that possible? As your soul prospers, so will your health and finances prosper.[18] That really encompasses your whole life in its entirety. I have found that learning to really enjoy your life is a key to a vibrantly healthy soul. The result will be a breakthrough of blessing in both finances and health. The whole person will benefit and thrive—a must for the happy prophet.

I grew up in an environment where serving God was more about the difficulties and hardships of life. It was looked upon as "suffering for Christ" and we were instructed to be a "good soldier"[19] through it all. The more spiritual you were, the worse pain you experienced. With this understanding, I would often fast ten days and be shaky and staggering around with a bad headache and no energy. This was supposed to be the sign of a true spiritual person. During my fasts I would pray for revival

---

[18] See 3 John 2.
[19] See 2 Tim 2:3.

three hours a day. Then after all that, I would go home and continue praying halfway through the night. My life was never about experiencing pleasure, but always about personal sacrifice.

Giving away my possessions to the poor and those in need was a top priority. I tithed regularly, contributed offerings on top of that, and gave away my own bicycle, clothes, shoes, and blankets to those who had much less. But, for all these efforts of generosity, I was not seeing the reward for my sacrificial giving.

I think as prophetic people, we can sometimes be very extreme. God honors sacrifice, but there comes a time when He wants to elevate us into a higher realm.

Be Generous to Yourself Also

One day I was complaining to the Lord about my lack of finances and the Christmas gifts I wasn't going to be able to purchase for my children. He told me, "Keith, you give away everything you receive." *Ouch.* I had just given away a hundred dollars someone had gifted me. It didn't even end up in my wallet! It came in one hand and went out the other. That had become my norm.

Then He told me, "You need to be generous."

I responded: "I am, Lord! I give away everything I have!"

I suddenly realized that what I thought was me being sacrificially generous by giving away what was given to me was actually *hurting* my financial situation and causing the lack. I wasn't stewarding well what God had so generously provided for all my needs.

He replied: "No, Keith . . . you need to be generous to *yourself.*"

You see, learning to be generous to yourself is learning to take good care of the vessel from which the Spirit and prophetic word flow. The Lord had also been speaking to me for a couple years about rest. But I didn't seem to be getting the point. He even gave me a prophetic word from someone with whom I didn't really have a good rapport. The word didn't even seem to fit the "encouragement" test for prophecy. Nevertheless, it was right on: "Keith, the Lord has been telling you to rest and you are late in receiving that word by six months." I knew he was right. Yet it took another six months for me to begin to understand what that meant.

Take Time for a "Hygge"

Shortly thereafter someone introduced me to the Danish word, *hygge,* pronounced, *hoo-ga.* It has to do with finding those things that really revitalize your heart and soul. These can be very simple things that create a restful and cozy environment, like lighting fragrant candles, logs burning in the fireplace, a quiet place in the garden, a cozy nook to snuggle up with a good book—whatever it is that brings a time of refreshing to you.

I was long overdue to implementing the word about rest the Lord had given me. It seemed I always had so many other things I was anxious to do. Sometimes prophetic people see the many things that need to be done—more territory to take, more battles to fight—that we actually don't know how to rest. My wife will occasionally remind me that I need to take on a different name besides "Keith" because my name means "meant for battle." At times she will say to me: "Do you always have to be looking for more territory to conquer? Do you not know how to rest?" And so I have been intentionally learning how to do just that—taking time to rest and recharge by implementing a *hygge*.

It has been sad for me to see so many prophetic ministers pass away over the last five years or so from a variety of serious physical conditions. It seems to me like they are dying prematurely. I wonder if part of it is the tendency we have to be so driven and focused that we lose sight of the simple joys of life. We have not learned how to truly find the enjoyment of life. Sadly, even I have to come to a tipping point at times before I'll listen and take heed to what the Lord is saying in regards to taking a much needed rest.

So I've been on a journey of discovering the things that I love to do that are for me a *hygge*. For instance, I really love to go to the redwood forests and just enjoy a quiet walk as I listen to the wind blowing through the tops of the trees, the sound of babbling streams, the chitter-chirping of birds, and the companionship and casual conversation with a friend who will sometimes join me.

Holy Spirit, my Helper, my Friend

I love worshiping the Lord and spending time with Him. He is my ultimate *hygge* and is a friend who is always nearby. One of the words for Holy Spirit is "Comforter", which is *parakletos* in the Greek.[20] It means, "advocate, intercessor, and consoler." The Holy Spirit is someone that comes alongside of us as a good friend. He is always in our court. He walks with us. He is our helper.

Eve was Adam's spouse, his helper, or "help meet"[21] as

---

[20]   Strong's Greek Lexicon, #G3875, "*parakletos*".
[21]   See Gen 2:18, KJV.

it says in the King James Version. God intended her to be his life-long companion and partner. She came alongside of him to help accomplish the task the Lord gave him. The Hebrew word that describes Eve as Adam's "help"-mate[22] means, "to surround"; "helper"; and, "aid"[23]. What a beautiful picture of the Holy Spirit.

The Rhythm of Life and Abiding Rest

In this most recent season of mine, I have been carrying two words: one is rest, and the other is returning back to our First Love. As soon as the Lord gave me both of those words, it seemed like I had more to do than ever. Everything I had been doing up to that time was great and good. It was all God-stuff: writing books (like this one), launching prophet schools, teaching, creating instructional videos, etc. All of these activities were necessary to expand the vision of developing prophets. But I've had to be much more intentional about my times of intimacy with the Lord and learn a restful rhythm so that in my hectic pace of ever-increasing ministry activities, I am able to maintain and work from a place of continual rest and refreshing. I asked Him, "How do I walk out both of those words?"

He put them together and replied, "Placing Me first as your First Love will result in an abiding rest." In that place of intimacy with the King is true rest. *Wonderful,* I thought. *I can do that.* Because He is truly my joy-source and holds the position of primary importance above anything else I *do* for Him.

---

[22] Strong's Hebrew concordance #H5828, "*ezer*".
[23] Gesenius' Hebrew-Chaldee Lexicon, #H5828; "*ezer*" is also described as "aid"; "a female helper".

As prophets, sometimes we can feel like it is our sole responsibility to save the world: we carry the weight of the world's issues on our shoulders, and with passionate urgency, we go after those things that prevent people from turning wholeheartedly back to God. In the busyness of these activities, we can lose our joy and lose out on the fullness of life as He intended.

One of the things I have had to fight for is keeping my family the number one priority. I'm glad to say that I have put measures in place to protect that. I would give up the prophetic ministry in a moment if it got in the way of my family. I don't enjoy traveling for ministry engagements more than being with my family. Besides the Lord, my family has truly become the greatest joy in my life, and that is a healthy place for every prophet to be.

The Joy of
Friendship

Fifteen

God gives family and good friends because we need to have both. I saw this on a plaque once:

Friends are family that you choose.

I like that because I've found it to be so true. The joy of friendship is another powerful key in our life. Prophets often have to overcome the lie of feeling alone. This is especially true during the early phases of developing the prophetic call.

Elijah felt alone and voiced it.

> *I am the **only one** of the LORD's prophets left . . .*
>
> 1 Kings 18:22a, emphasis added

He seemed to have forgotten, however, the recent conversation with the prophet Obadiah who told him he had been hiding 100 prophets.

> *Haven't you heard, my lord, what I did while Jezebel was killing the prophets of the LORD? I hid a hundred of the LORD's prophets in two caves, fifty in each, and supplied them with food and water.*
>
> 18:13

In his own personal loneliness, it seems like Elijah didn't even hear what Obadiah said because he complains to the Lord:

> *I am the only one left, and now they are trying to kill me too.*
>
> 1 Kings 19:14b

The "I'm All Alone"-Complex

In the often solitary walk of a prophet, we can sometimes have an "all alone"-complex. I know I have had one. Loneliness, and feeling alone, is a sure way to lose joy. If you don't have anyone to share life with, you can definitely feel very alone. I didn't realize I had a spirit of loneliness until I started being attacked for a long season with ungodly thoughts, which I could not shake. I knew they weren't right, but for months I was oppressed by these thoughts.

Finally, the Lord told me that those thoughts were not the real issue. The thoughts were coming because of the bigger lie: *You're all alone.* So I had to begin to war against those lies with declarations of truth:

I am not an orphan, I am a son.

I am not alone any longer. Christ is with me.

I have a loving wife who loves to be with me.

I have wonderful children who like to be with me.

I had to war with one of my favorite scriptural truths:

Because you are his sons, God sent the Spirit of his Son into our hearts, the Spirit who calls out, "Abba, Father." So you are no longer a slave, but God's child; and since you are his child, God has made you also an heir.

Galatians 4:6-7

Praise the Lord that we are no longer orphans! He lives in us. We are not alone, He is not alone, we are a family. And as His family, we have an inheritance. That's such good news.

I've always had people that like me, and I've had many people who call me their good friend. But you can be surrounded by people all the time with lots of activity going on, yet when you get a few minutes to yourself, you still feel so all alone.

My wife has always been great at connecting with other gals as friends. They enjoy just hanging out and having fun. But for many years, I've had a hard time doing that. I'm great at making ministry friends and mentoring relationships. But one thing the Lord has been teaching me in this past season is the value of friendship. All sustainable breakthroughs have to come from the Lord, and He was leading me to that place to appreciate its value even more.

My friend, the King

A couple of years ago as I began to press into gaining more understanding about friendship, I told the Lord I wanted to get one thing from Him that year: *His* friendship. I wanted to learn to be a friend of the Lord. It started me on a great journey. You see, I was really good at receiving Him as Dad/Father, Provider, and Protector. But being a friend and knowing Him as a friend was different. I started to get the revelation that He really wanted to be *my* friend. That alone was awesome to consider. To be the friend of the King of kings is no light matter. I imagined myself sitting across from Him talking about the issues of this world that were on His heart. You know, He cares about the seven billion people on this planet, and He knows each one by name! *That* King wants to be *my* friend! Usually friends are on the same level as peers. But I am fully cognizant that in this relationship, the King of the universe, the Savior of the whole world—this great God far above my level—is inviting *me* into a deeper more intimate eternal *friendship*. Jesus extended the same invitation to His disciples:

> *I no longer call you servants, because a servant does not know his master's business. Instead, I have called you friends, for everything that I learned from my Father I have made known to you.*

> John 15:15

God was bringing me into a much more intimate relationship with Him, and I took it. As I sat in His presence, I could see myself looking Him in the eyes as we exchanged powerful conversations. That is what is really in His heart—to enter into a deeper friendship with us than we even think is possible.

As I began to grow more comfortable in my friendship with Him, I asked Him for the same kind of friendship connections in my life. I didn't just want relationships built around a particular ministerial function; I had spent years doing that. I had lots of friends connected to me because I was a pastor, a prophet, a minister, or part of the church leadership. When I wasn't functioning in those roles, however, the relationships weren't there either, because they weren't built on a deeper foundation. If my relationships were solely based on function, then when we weren't joined in that role, there was no friendship. I really wanted friends with whom I could enjoy life.

Developing Healthy and Genuine Friendships

Being friendless can be a huge joy killer. But having genuine friends who care about you personally, regardless of the roles you play, is an important part of experiencing contentment and fulfillment in life. As prophets grow in influence, they will often find people who relate to them around their gift. At first, they mistake the specialized attention as a desire for friendship, because more often than not, prophets have experienced their share of rejection, loneliness, and lack of affirmation. So this extra attention can be misinterpreted. A prophet's gift can lead them into relationships where they receive a lot of attention and notoriety. But it is only a false sense of satisfaction that doesn't last long. Very soon they are feeling frustrated, and used, and sometimes taken advantage of. But people desire friends who simply enjoy them for who they are, not just for what they do. That's why it is vital to seek to build healthy relationships beyond your gifting in hopes it will develop into true friendship.

As I have progressed deeper into this friendship revelation, I was contending for healthy connections. I went after relationships with guys who were close in age, not to do ministry, but just to hang out. There were times when a friend and I considered doing ministry together, but the Lord would say, "Could you build this connection on recreation and not on ministry?" So, we would set aside the ministry idea, because I have plenty of ministry connections. What was missing in my life were healthy friendships that bring refreshment and rest. With such established friendships, we will struggle less with an "alone" complex.

Remember, we are going after sustainable joy, and joy comes in family and genuine friendships and being known by people with whom we have a history in all the good, the bad, and even the ugly of our life.

I am thankful to say that I have been finding more and more joy in my own pursuit of genuine friendships. My wife and I love to get together with friends who really know how to have fun and who also enjoy good food! It is great to have ministry friends who share the same giftings and ministry objectives, but I also like *fun* friends. These are ones with whom you can laugh easily, go out for a nice evening and enjoy a great time together where you don't have to appear religious or perfect or polished. With fun friends, you don't have to have it all together! You can let your hair down, so to speak, be yourself, and just enjoy one another's company. There's no pressure to exercise your gift. Everyone needs the kind of friends who love God, but who also know how to just hang together and enjoy life.

Friends Doing Life Together

Life is too short to be continually consumed with the countless urgent needs of humanity. They will still be there tomorrow: the poor, the abused, those in need of healing, issues that demand attention, problems needing solutions, words from the Lord to unpack and walk out, and so on. It's necessary to regularly take time to recharge so we can function most fully for all that is required of us over the long haul. The best way to do this as we walk life's journey is in the company of good friends.

One of the keys to developing healthy friendships is knowing it takes time to cultivate great relationships. I have discovered that I sometimes don't hit it off right away with someone. It seems I am slow to warm up, because at times, I am a bit suspicious when I first meet someone. I feel that, perhaps, we are both sizing up one another and it's a bit uncomfortable. But now I give myself and the other person grace in that first stage of relationship. As I stick with it, over the course of time I will come to see some great attributes in that person that I find really valuable and fun. Sometimes we find a friendship we're pursuing just isn't a good fit. That's okay. Still I continue to go after friendships, because staying in the relational game is really important to me.

I have also learned that to have friends I must be willing to pursue the relationship. I can't just sit around hoping someone will call me. I have to go after the friendship by demonstrating friendliness.

> *A man that hath friends must shew himself friendly.*
>
> Proverbs 18:24, KJV

I may even need to initiate the first move to pursue the relationship. I also have to smile and act friendly! I know that sounds funny, but sometimes prophets hide behind their life-is-so-serious attitude because it's most familiar to them. Whereas smiling and being friendly and approachable won't happen if you're suspicious of people, thinking you won't be understood for who you are. Sometimes prophets even feel people are talking about them, believing everyone is against them, and that they are the only one truly set apart to God and His purposes. I know many that feel this way, and at times, I have, too. It is not the truth, of course, but sometimes it can *feel* that way. Those negative and untrue thoughts must be dismantled, and in the face of these temptations to disconnect, you must instead *pursue connection* with people.

Don't expect your friendships to be perfect if you haven't taken the time to nurture the relationship, and don't expect them to be great if you haven't communicated your own needs. Sometimes I hear prophetic people complain about how they're not being valued in a relationship. I then inquire if they took time to communicate what they need. Oftentimes they don't want to share or they've shared in a harsh or an insensitive way. Relationships take skill, and this is an area of weakness for many prophetic people. Perhaps in twenty years it won't be a big issue with prophets, but right now, prophets and prophetic people can sometimes appear as if they are anti-church, anti-relationships, and anti-social. The truth is that those with a prophetic gift haven't felt safe in church, in relationships, or society, in general, and so it presents more of a challenge to them as they move out of their own comfort zone. They are often misunderstood, and that may be because they don't know how to communicate in a healthy way at the proper time and in an appropriate manner. I know I haven't. But I'm thankful that I am learning and making progress.

All these efforts are so worth it, because I have come to really value friendship and truly enjoy quality time with my friends. I believe the same will be true for you as you invest your best efforts in friendships.

Disengage and
Enjoy Life

Sixteen

Prophets are particularly known for their sensitivity; it is what makes them stand apart. One of the reasons prophets find it difficult to enjoy themselves in a public setting is that they don't know how to turn off their spiritual antennas. They keep their radar on all the time where they are constantly feeling things, knowing things, acknowledging things, seeing things, etc. They don't realize that they also need to learn to just enjoy life and have a good time. This is actually an intentional choice we must make.

My very patient wife has had to endure many years with a husband who is also a prophet with a hypersensitivity to the environment all around. We would go on a nice vacation in a foreign country, and I'd be warring with the spirit in that region. I've had that happen a number of times. I know they are valid experiences, but I wish I had also learned how to disengage when I needed to. After all, we are not called to battle every war we encounter, only Spirit-directed ones.

On one of our vacations on foreign soil, I remember being tormented for days on end. Finally on the very last day, I saw the demon responsible.

"I never want to see you in this country ever again!" he threatened menacingly.

But that only stirred up a holy fire within me and I announced aloud, "Oh, I'll be back! You can *count* on it!"

While it is true that we don't always get to determine what is happening to us in the spirit realm, I think there are some tools that would help us know when it is our time to war in the spirit and when it is simply time to enjoy life. Times of intentional rest, like a family vacation, would be one of those.

I remember going through a season of being supersensitive to everything. I would go into a restaurant and the hostess would seat us. But shortly thereafter, I had to ask her to move us because I was picking up something from the person behind us that made me cautious and alert in the spirit. There came a point when I finally said, "Enough! I want to enjoy myself when I go out and I am not going to have the spirit realm rule me."

Here is an important key: we are called to rule our gift.

> *The spirits of prophets are subject to the control of prophets.*
>
> 1 Corinthians 14:32

There comes a time when we have to recognize that the devil is overplaying his hand and we must announce to the spirit realm: "Enough is enough!" We are the ones who quiet down what we are sensing to allow ourselves a much-needed time-out in order to facilitate a rest. If we are always dialed up, then the ones we love will feel ignored and uncared for. They need us to be fully engaged with them and not always giving our attention to the spiritual atmosphere around us.

Supersensitive from an unhealthy place = Suspicion

A friend was telling me a theory of his in a recent conversation. He ministers to people all over the world in inner healing. He said he noticed that the prophets who are supersensitive to everything often gained their sensitivity to the spirit realm because they were not healthy growing up. They may have been abused, misused, overlooked, abandoned, etc. The difficulties of their upbringing made them supersensitive. That gave them their ability to see and feel in the spirit, but with it also came life's wounds. So his goal was to get them healed so they still could walk in their gift, but not from a supersensitive unhealthy place.

I remember early on I was mostly suspicious of people. I was always looking out for the evils in the heart of man and focused on people's tendencies to control, betray, or reject. This caused me to always be warning those I cared about concerning such untrustworthy people. My woundings and supersensitivity came from being raised in the Church. I had seen people hurt my parents deeply in the name of God while claiming to be good Christians. I believe those incidents planted the seeds of suspicion about people in church, that they couldn't be trusted. I even had an *expectation* that they would one day wound me also, or at least, someone I know. Eventually I did experience some of the same wounds I had seen my parents go through. And as I did, I carried these wounds into my own pastorate with a belief system that said: *You can't trust church people! They will hurt you!* In order to get healed, I had to go after the root of the real problem. I had to fight my way to changing this untrue belief system to one that chose to believe people are basically *good* and they aren't looking to betray me. Even though I have had a few betrayals along the way, I discovered more and more that people do have a lot of good in them, and that became my primary focus instead of negative human characteristics.

Develop Your Vision with the Father's Lens

I have enjoyed being around some great leaders who have modeled seeing the good in people, including the good in me! The more I am around these kind of individuals, the more I begin to also alter my own thought patterns. It is amazing that when I look for the negative in someone, I will most *always* find it. But focusing on a person's bad side is so overrated, and people always have some characteristic or pattern of behavior that is being transformed.

Part of my gifting as a life coach is to find the constraints that are hindering breakthroughs. Identifying these is the success of one being a great carrier of personal and corporate breakthrough. We must see where the bottleneck is. But not recognizing that this ability is a gift from God will eventually cause us to function in an unhealthy manner. I am always seeing the places that need more breakthroughs. I see where things are and where they need to be.

To Engage . . . or Not Engage

I have had to be trained by the Lord and others to see when I am functioning in an unhealthy way, however. The times when I have gotten myself into trouble and lost much sleep and my joy is when I go after a breakthrough in someone where God has not given me permission to do so.

To prevent this, I have put safety measures in place to ensure I have God's go-ahead by asking key questions:

- Am I the one who is supposed to be dealing with this person's issue?

- Is this an area/region where I am called to bring breakthrough? If the answer is "no," then I must leave it alone.

As my friend, Dano McCollam, often says, "The gift can work all the time, but it works best somewhere specifically." Learning to know where God wants me to release the breakthrough gift is key. I know that wherever I go, breakthrough usually follows. I will see staff situations altered, finances change, businesses advance into blessings, and churches transition in growth and size. Usually whatever negative thing is there will be exposed. If there is a reward due, it comes through. If there are hidden issues there, they come to light. It is the nature of breakthrough, and it is what I love to do.

But at times, this breakthrough gift can also steal my joy. When I get involved with someone I'm not supposed to help, I set myself up for a difficult trial. That is why it is good to ask yourself these questions first:

- Has God directed me to help this person or to speak prophetically into their life at this time?

- Do I have His permission to speak into them?

Just because you see clearly what is going on in a person's life and can also see where the breakthrough is doesn't mean you have God's permission to go after the issue. Learning the difference between initiating the operation of your gift and the Lord leading you specifically through your gift is key. I can always see in the spirit, but it does not necessarily mean it is an assignment to be activated at this time.

When I am with my family, it is not the time to deal with every spiritual atmosphere I'm sensing. Sometimes the enemy tries to distract us and gets us stirred up by igniting a negative atmosphere. Sometimes we just step into a negative atmosphere that someone else stirred up. Learning how to ignore it when it isn't our assignment and just live life is most often the best warfare tool you can utilize.

There are times when the warfare is so intense and you are feeling the weightiness of the enemy, and the best strategy may be to just go watch a good clean, funny movie. There are other times when I have to stop trying to engage the Lord in the spirit realm because it doesn't seem to be getting anywhere. In that moment I need to go out and play basketball with my son or go get something to eat with my daughter. I find that when I do reengage the situation in the spirit, I have what I need to follow through.

Picking up Someone Else's Offense

Have you ever been tormented by the injustice of how someone is treating another person? I have. That injustice will rise up in me sometimes for weeks on end. Once I hear how a person is wronging others, then I am on the watch for other transgressions that person makes. Inevitably, I will soon hear about another incident where that same person mistreated someone else, and I get more and more agitated. At that point I look for an opportunity to come at this situation head on. *After all,* I say to myself, *I am God's prophet. Aren't I called to address these kinds of injustices? Don't I see what's happening with my own eyes? Because I see it, doesn't it mean I have to deal with it by confronting them?*

This is where I have gotten myself in the most trouble. It is like an offense that builds up in me until I just can't hold it in any longer. It will come gushing out in the wrong place to the wrong person at the wrong time, and boom! An offense bomb explodes right there where I suddenly find myself engaged in a huge confrontation. Joy has left the building, as did the joy in my heart. And all this because I allowed someone else's offense to take root in me under the guise of protecting truth and fighting for justice.

Learning to not take on other's offenses is a skill we must master. One of the things I've had to learn is to tell the offended person not to give me any information about how so-and-so hurt them. I don't want to hear it. I have had to stop them, even if they are a close friend. I also have to be careful not to inadvertently lead someone to freely share his or her problems about a particular person. I know that once they have shared it, those offenses often become stuck in my spirit and I can't dislodge them. Every time I see that person after that, it is only through the lens of the offense. Unfortunately, this kind of thing is all too common, and if allowed free rein, it will be like a terminal disease that will consume and steal all of your joy and peace.

A Prophet of Justice and Mercy

Learning not to take the bait of the offense in the first place is crucial. Don't even take a nibble. As prophetic people, we are, indeed, people of justice. More than anything, we are passionate for truth to prevail. But as we grow in the Lord, we have to realize that more often than not, Kingdom justice is best demonstrated through mercy. I like how the prophet Zechariah says it:

> *This is what the LORD Almighty said: "Administer true justice; show mercy and compassion to one another."*
>
> 7:9

Finding ways to release mercy and kindness to people through acts of compassion instead of responding with righteous indignation and angry frustration is the true Kingdom way. Those negative emotions are such joy stealers. We get angry when we see how people have fallen short of a Kingdom principle. *Aren't they supposed to be walking in that truth?* we say. *Don't they know better?* We get more and more upset because we, of course, are upholding the *true* standards of His Word. When in reality, we are judging them and heaping judgment upon ourselves in the process. In the end, we are the ones losing, because those who refuse to extend mercy walk around joyless and miserable. Meanwhile, the other person is completely unaware that their issue is tormenting us, unless, of course, we open our mouth and give them a piece of our mind by spewing emotionally-charged words. But that is not wisdom, nor is it productive. In fact, it's the fastest way to find yourself right back at the bottom of the joyless pit having to go through a whole new set of learning experiences all over again. When we blast judgmental words about an injustice instead of administering mercy, we set ourselves way back to square one.

Saying the Right Thing at the Right Time

I have seen too many frustrated prophets who are wondering why they are not being received and heard. Timing is huge. You can be saying the right thing at the wrong time and wonder how come no one is hearing you or responding appropriately. Believe me, I have said the right thing at the wrong way too many times. Sometimes I have said the right thing at the wrong time. Other times I have said the wrong thing at the wrong time. Each of these are recipes for disaster.

The key is learning how to know when you have the go-ahead to engage and give the message, and when to step aside and disengage to just enjoy life. Joy will always be found as you stay in step with the peaceable leading of the Holy Spirit.

Wisdom Releases Joy

Seventeen

There's such joy as a happy and healthy prophet learns the lessons wisdom teaches. Discovering when to release what God is showing you and how to release it brings great contentment to your heart, and where there is contentment, joy is close at hand.

As a prophet, you often have the privilege to see where things are supposed to be and what God wants to do. Then you have the charge of Heaven to wait patiently until His word comes to pass.

> *Brothers and sisters, as an example of patience in the face of suffering, take the prophets who spoke in the name of the Lord. As you know, we count as blessed those who have persevered. You have heard of Job's perseverance and have seen what the Lord finally brought about. The Lord is full of compassion and mercy.*
>
> James 5:10-11

Our task is to remain patient as the word is released and until it is received. But if we don't know how to walk in patience and joy in these situations, then we are going to be frustrated, disillusioned, and ultimately, an unhealthy, unhappy prophet.

When to Speak a Word

Sometimes I am invited to a church, a gathering, leadership teams, etc., because they desire prophetic insight. Sometimes the things I see in the spirit prophetically and what people are able to receive are two vastly different things. Believe me, I know the frustration of God showing me where the people should be compared to where they are at present. When I release the things that I see but the people are not ready to hear it, I know I'm headed for big trouble with a long and arduous journey ahead. Subsequently, I have decidedly joined myself to the task of learning when to speak the word and when to wait. Speaking the right word at the wrong time never has a good end, and then I must deal with the inevitable painful result because of my lack of wisdom.

I remember once I was asked to speak prophetically into a team. Now I've shared this story in another context, but I want to share it again here. I clearly saw specific changes that needed to be made in this team, but I knew it wasn't the right thing to say, at least not then. But the team kept pressing me. They perceived there was something more and that I was holding back. So they pressed further urging me to tell *everything*. Unwisely, I took the grenade, pulled the pin, and dropped it in that meeting room.

"You need to make a change in your leadership team," I told them.

Boom. The silence that followed was deafening. I went on to add, "Several people in this room need some adjustments." With this announcement, I began to call out their names and told each one what I thought should happen. Boom. Boom. Boom.

Later I learned that for the previous two years, other prophets had been saying something very similar to that team. At the moment when I released that little bombshell-word, there was no more wondering what should be done with their team. It was crystal clear. But it was definitely painful, for them and for me. The leaders weren't ready to make such a radical decision. From that moment on, I knew it was going to get ugly. Needless to say I didn't have a pleasant drive to the airport with the pastor's wife the next day. *I had just blown her little world apart.*

It took a few months for this leadership team to recover, but they did. Meanwhile, I felt so bad for all that transpired that for months and even years after, every time I saw a member of this team, I went through pangs of guilt. *How could I have done that?* My mind would replay that meeting room scenario over and over and it pained me afresh each time.

Such difficult learning experiences will, in time, mature prophets as lessons of wisdom are gained.

Wait . . . Test the Timing

Even if you feel something so strong in your gut, I have learned that if I wait a few days, it will often lift. Usually when I leave the geographic region where I've been, it lifts, and then I am so thankful I didn't blurt out the word I felt *so intensely* at the time. Sometimes, God will lead me to give that same word at a later time, and it will be well received. Why? Because the timing was right. By the time I do deliver it, I am not feeling the pressure of urgency. Sometimes after the pressure has lifted, the timing will be right to give it. So, it comes down to restraining the urge to give a word until you are assured of the release to give it, and this takes time to learn.

Whenever you give a word outside of the right time, you're going to experience frustration with yourself and the situation. The enemy loves to capitalize on that mistake and attempt to make you feel guilty by assaulting your mind again and again about how wrong you were. In such times, joy is nowhere to be found.

Release Personal Ownership of the Word

It can be frustrating for prophets when others do not receive the word of the Lord, and because we honor His word so much, it feels like a personal attack. We can unwisely begin to take personal ownership of a word by attaching expectations of timing and responses where, when they are not met, we lose our joy. But we must remember, it is God's word, not ours. It is our responsibility to deliver it and His responsibility to perform it. We have to learn that He has given us that word and then we have to release it and return it back to Him. If people do not receive it, well then, we will consider how to deliver it through another expression until it is received readily or until God chooses to give it again through someone else.

The prophet Samuel was told by God to anoint Saul to be the king of Israel. We're familiar with the story. Saul readily received this word. But not too long after, he did not respond correctly to another word of the Lord, which caused God to grieve that he even had made Saul king. As a result, the word of the Lord changed and God chose David to be king instead. Without a doubt this unexpected outcome was a frustrating challenge for the prophet.

As prophets we have to realize that even as the word of the Lord is delivered, God honors a person's free will. They have a choice to honor the word of the Lord or not. If they do not receive the word and obey it, like King Saul, then God will find someone else who will honor His word.

The result following our delivery of the word may be very different than we expected. A wise prophet prepares himself for the unexpected outcome.

Waiting for the Change . . . in Joy!

It can be quite frustrating when year in and year out a church receives the same word of the Lord, the same challenge, but they are slow to step into it. A prophet can feel personally rejected, not received, hurt by the inaction, and wondering why they aren't joyfully jumping into what God made so clear. But at the end of the day, it really is more about what God is doing in you than what He is doing in everyone else. We must remind ourselves again that we are not responsible for how the people respond to the word of the Lord, and if we're focused on their receptivity, we will spend many years frustrated.

Change in a local church or team can happen very slowly, and we must be patient as God works in them. Maintaining a joyful heart in the process of God working in the midst of His people will be much more productive in the long term. What is God doing, meanwhile? He's releasing His goodness to them in ways that position them to receive His word and bolsters courage to make the necessary changes for the sake of His Kingdom.

Joyful prophets are those who know how good God is and that He is looking for those who will respond affirmatively to His word. We are called to scatter His word like seed. If it is not received, then we must guard ourselves against harboring anger that may try to rise up in response. Negative emotions do not produce love, joy, and peace, but will instead lead us back to hiding out in our cave, like Elijah did, away from the very people to whom we are called to speak.

In the Right Spirit

I have to trust that God will let my words be released in a way that is going to bring the greatest impact. Remember, He will not let His Word return back void. If we are patient and stay joyfully consistent, we will have the ear of those willing to do all that is necessary to implement the word of the Lord in its time. But if our pattern is to respond in frustration when people do not receive what we bring, then we will deliver His word in the wrong spirit and we'll feel the backlash. People sense frustration and know when you're responding to them negatively. This is something we have to go after with the Lord so that we always speak His word in the right spirit—in love. That is the language of Heaven and the only language we must speak to deliver His message. Without love, His word is communicated in a tone that is too harsh for people to take it to heart.

This can be a challenge too—bringing a word in love— because you have passionately carried it for so long. It becomes so personal to you that it is like a baby growing inside of you. It's difficult for you to even release this word because it's been so much a part of you. You long for others to honor what has been growing in you for so long. Anything less feels dishonoring and can cause us to respond in the wrong spirit.

That is why I believe God is raising up companies of prophets in these days. A prophet needs to have a place where others understand who you are, knows what you carry, and will extend grace and love that encourages you. A company of prophets helps each other grow and mature in their gift within a safe environment, and lends courage where needed to release the message in the right spirit.

Whatever You Preach You Empower

We have to be careful what we do with the things we have seen in the spirit and not be too hasty to share it. For instance, one time I saw the enemy and what he was doing. When I shared publicly what I was seeing, I actually empowered what he was doing, so that in a boomerang effect, it returned back to hit me. I literally came under the same attack of the enemy I just preached to expose! Later on, God had to teach me that just because you see what the enemy is doing, doesn't mean you preach it. A key to remember: **Whatever you preach, you empower.** He taught me how to speak to that which needed to be cultivated. For example, if I want to see a culture of forgiveness despite the fact that bitterness prevailed in the atmosphere, I must speak about a culture of mercy and forgiveness. In this way I am describing how Heaven operates instead of highlighting the ways of the dominion of darkness. It doesn't mean I can't expose what the enemy is doing and speak to that, but I need to do it in a context where people are activated with courageous hope that overcomes the enemy, not simply recognize and give place to his destructive activities.

But is it the Correct Interpretation?

I've had serious backlash when I released what I saw but with an incorrect interpretation. The right interpretation concerning what you see in the spirit is imperative and so necessary for an impactful Kingdom connection with people.

Once I was invited into a church to speak in an evening meeting. All I could see in that meeting was an elder brother spirit. I then spoke to the elder brother spirit when I preached. As I did, I was subtly directing it to a specific individual in that meeting. Sometimes we don't even realize we are doing that. But later on I realized that this same spirit was on several of the leadership team and a few church members as well. The way I released the word stirred up suspicion in the team. They finally asked me, "Who do you see specifically as the one carrying this elder brother spirit?" I shared who I thought it was and the pastor asked me to speak to the person directly about it.

I thought I was helping out, but I was really hurting the whole situation because I did not see it fully or have enough relational equity to personally deal with it. Yes, there were issues going on with this person, but I was only seeing in part. That incident took about two years to clean up where relationships were finally restored to a good place.

Sometimes when you look back on such incidents, you realize if you had said something in a different way, you would have brought people together instead of causing discord and division. This was one of those times, and it was a hard lesson of wisdom.

Enlarge the Solution, Not the Problem

Speak to the problem and increase the problem. Speak to the solution and release the solution. Whenever I have spoken to the problem, I have released a season of intense stress on my life. When there is stress, there is no joy. Instead you are frustrated, hurt, confused, shamed, and a whole host of other negative emotions. It is not a good place to live.

Learning the wisdom of timing, rightly releasing a word from the Lord in the right spirit, and waiting patiently in joy are essential keys to victory.

Laughter
Instead of
Worry

Eighteen

Staying preoccupied and consumed with God's goodness, instead of focusing on the big issues of concern that demand our attention is key for a happy and joy-filled prophet. It's cause for much more spontaneous laughter and joy in our life.

Years ago, I found myself in a really frustrated spot when I was pastoring. Hearing about this, my pastor and prophet friend, Dan McCollam, called me and I spent the first several minutes detailing how I didn't like this and that problem going on in my church. I told him about my frustration with certain individuals, the financial situation was an increasing worry, etc. On and on I went, listing my anxious and frustrated concerns in my church. He quietly listened to me for a while and then I heard laughter erupting from the other end of the line. *He's laughing at me!* I thought. *How could he? Doesn't he know what I'm going through and how difficult this is for me? What kind of friend is that??*

But actually, it was exactly what I needed at that moment, and I knew it even though I didn't *feel* it. In fact, I was feeling everything *but* laughter. Slowly, slowly though, I too, began to laugh . . . just to appease him at first . . . you know, a courtesy laugh. Have you ever done that? Well I did, and it worked! Sometimes you make the first move toward a breakthrough and the next thing you know, boom! God shows up. It didn't take long before I was rolling on the floor laughing hysterically, facedown on the ground, with Dano still on the phone. Now we were both laughing hard. It was then that I heard the Lord speak, "Keith, it's supposed to be easy and fun."

Well, it wasn't . . . but God was changing my perspective.

Enter into a Greater Reality

Sometimes the best thing a prophet can do when he is feeling the weight of life's pressures is to stop what he's doing and yield to the goodness of God. Take a good look and really see it. Initiating a time of thanksgiving and erupting in joyful laughter is a doorway that causes you to enter into heavenly reality.

> Enter his gates with thanksgiving and his courts with praise; give thanks to him and praise his name.
>
> Psalm 100:4

To live in those heavenly realities we must intentionally choose to thank Him while simultaneously choosing to let go of whatever circumstances we've been focused on. Turn your eyes away from those concerns and upwards toward the greater reality. As we begin to thank the Lord for what He is doing in our midst, joy is the natural result. Thanksgiving turns on the faucet for the overflow.

I remember a specific time when I prayed for revival for months on end. God stopped me one day in the middle of a three-hour prayer session and said, "Son, I want you to start thanking Me for what I am doing in your midst."

As I did, joy began to just pour out of me. I could then see very specifically what He was doing in our community: *We are being revived; souls are being saved; people are being healed!* I could see that, indeed, God was already moving. From that moment on, my whole perspective changed and I was overjoyed. Thanksgiving is like putting on a pair of eyeglasses that helps us see with Heaven's vision God's goodness right there in front of us. It was there all along, but if you don't intentionally look for it, you won't see it. Thanksgiving will open our eyes and unlock the abundance readily available once you apprehend it.

> *Then some boats from Tiberias landed near the place where the people had eaten the bread after the Lord had given thanks.*
>
> John 6:23

The bread and fish were multiplied and fed to the multitudes *after* Jesus gave thanks. Giving thanks to God opens up Heaven's reality even during frustrating circumstances. The answer may be closer than you think. Why worry about it when you can get filled up with joy? Let your mouth be filled with laughter instead!

There is a time to pray, a time to bring to birth, and a time to grieve, and a time to laugh,[24] and then there is a time to look for what God is doing in your circumstance and offer Him thanks. Remember, thanksgiving is looking for what God is already doing and then rejoicing over it.

If you can see it, then you can see it multiplied.

Elijah had to learn this. The prophet crouched down and bent way over to pray for rain in a season of severe

---

[24] See Eccl 3:4.

drought. After a while he directed his servant, "Go . . . look for rain."[25] It took seven times, but by the seventh time, his servant saw a very small cloud. That was enough for Elijah; he was just looking for a smidge of breakthrough.

He then prophesied, "The rain is coming!" he told Ahab the king. "Hurry, or else it will overtake you."

Sure enough, the rain came, and it came down in torrents. Finally, the long drought was over as the dam of blessing burst forth in a deluge.

Joyful Expectation

As prophets, our job is to share, pray, or declare something that we know God wants to do. But we have to also wait expectantly in faith for the answers to come, even in its seed form. If we don't, our hearts will get sick with discouragement and hopelessness.

> *Hope deferred makes the heart sick . . .*
>
> Proverbs 13:12a

When we feel like God is not going to move on our behalf, we start losing the joyful expectation that something good is coming our way. To counter this, begin to look for a sign of the tangible evidence—however small—that He is answering your prayers. It's there . . . keep looking. Then celebrate it—I mean, really celebrate! Make it a joy-party with a lot of laughter. Invite your family . . . your friends. Tell the testimonies of God's goodness. Then laugh some more. Once you've celebrated, watch that small seed grow as you wait patiently in more joyful expectation for its full maturity. It's coming.

---

[25] See 1 Kings 18:41-19:8.

Ignore, Ignore

There are times when my wife, Heather, and I are in the midst of a warfare atmosphere. It doesn't feel good, that's for sure. What battle does? But we must determine and plan ahead of time what we are going to do in such times. A good strategy for staying above the schemes of the enemy is to go do something fun. In the middle of the warfare, we may feel like we should be praying or crying or worrying, but instead, we choose to ignore it! Because the best strategy, in some situations, is to simply ignore the enemy and let God fight the battle. To do this, Heather and I go out for a nice meal, watch a movie, go for a drive, or just hang out with fun friends. By choosing to play and have fun, and maybe even laugh at ourselves, we ignore those little annoyances of the enemy's distraction tactics that trigger negative emotions and get us both worked up. In doing so, we are intentionally ignoring him and refusing to take his bait, which really annoys him.

Breaking Through the Impasse

Choosing to focus on God's goodness with thanksgiving is a powerful tool in our arsenal and positions us to receive all we need to be strengthened and encouraged in the midst of the battle. He's winning it anyway, and we get to enjoy the process by implementing a joy-activity, like a good laugh time!

As prophets, sometimes we don't know how to let up from boring down full force on an issue at hand. We can be like a pit bull who latches on to its prey and refuses to let go. His teeth are locked into place. That is a good characteristic most often, but at other times, we have to know when to let go and let God take care of issues that consume our time, drain our resources, and put a strain on our emotions.

When you are in a battle, you sometimes need an intervention. Have you ever been in that place of disagreement with someone you care about? It doesn't matter what you say, it just doesn't go right. *That is warfare.* In such times, you need to enlist a trusted intercessor to intervene on your behalf.

Years ago, Heather and I were engaged in such a battle, arguing endlessly back and forth, and we just couldn't see our way out. We asked an intercessor friend to pray for us. As she did, she could see in the spirit that we were in a room with no outlet. She started praying and busted that thing loose. The enemy loves to imprison us with no seeming way of escape.

It is important that we recognize when we need to request help in spiritual battles, especially an impasse. Learning to let go of the pressing issue at hand and backing off for a time is often just what is needed to bring a resolution. As a fighter, I *never* want to let go; I'm firmly fixed on the battle to victory. But I have learned that sometimes the best strategy to winning the fight is to choose a timeout. Take a break. Go get some rest. It is like having to power down your computer before the software can be upgraded. When the computer powers back up, the operating system is initialized and the new software version loads successfully. That is how it is for us. Sometimes we have to completely power down, shut off, unwind, ignore, stop fighting, and take a timeout. Then, when we do get back in the game, we realize that things aren't quite the way we thought they were. We take on a very different perspective. With clear eyes, we have a fresh new vision and will have gained a higher wisdom with understanding on how to ensure victory as we reengage the situation.

From Joy to Joy

A healthy and happy prophet exchanges worry and anxiety for joy and laughter along the path of life that leads from glory to glory, strength to strength, and joy to joy. Implementing thanksgiving, praise, and much more spontaneous laughter are essential for the New Covenant prophet to press right on through to the finish.

Remember!

Nineteen

The ability to sustain the encounters God gives you is to remember all He has done, and then recall it again and again. In fact, the power to remember is heightened as we testify about specific accounts from the past and bring those into the present. For this reason God gave His prophets a memory.

> *Worship God! For the testimony of Jesus is the spirit of prophecy.*
>
> Revelation 19:10, NKJV

Testimony is when we utilize our memory to recall the blessings and all the good things God has done for us, and it is the best way to employ the power of our God-given memory. Doing so will keep joy tangible in our life.

If you respond with laugher in a Holy Ghost-encounter (something you need to do often!) but have difficulty keeping a positive perspective on life, then joy is not yet well established in your life, and it makes you vulnerable to enemy attack. Joy is so much more than a laughing encounter; it is the response of remembering God in His goodness and foundational for keeping us prophets sharp and alert to heavenly realities.

Your Enemy Lies

The enemy, on the other hand, is good at reminding us of the negative things of our past, and he especially loves to remind us of our failures. He also loves to stir us up by reminding us of things that went wrong, people who didn't receive us, challenges we didn't overcome, our disqualifications, and loss. He uses the power of memory as a tactic *against us* by reminding us of all the ways we are incompetent, and brings up painful things locked away in our memory. It is his attempt to obscure the present victory in our life and move us to a state of hopelessness, thereby immobilizing us. He likes to suggest: "Things didn't change before, and they certainly won't change now. It's all so hopeless. What's the use?"

But he is a liar and a defeated foe.

The Power of Testimony

To challenge him we must be aggressive in utilizing the power of our testimony by recalling the victories God has brought. **We must *remember* His goodness!** The testimony is the spirit of prophecy shouting aloud its declaration: "If God did it back then, He will do it again!" Amen.

This is the place from where we prophesy. When I prophesy over a person, I do so because I have confidence in the many prophetic words I have released over people's lives that opened up a breakthrough opportunity for them and brought dramatic change. Testimony reminds me that prophecy is, and has been, effective.

I remember being in a really difficult season financially. The house loans were eating me alive; I was late in paying the bills and barely keeping things afloat. I felt like I was spinning many plates simultaneously trying to keep the creditors at bay, especially with the high interest rates at that time. Meanwhile, God was teaching me a lot about His faithfulness. But I had been going through this battle for eight months, and frankly, I was worn out. It didn't seem like there was any conceivable way that I could get a financial breakthrough. In fact, it looked like I was losing.

So, God instructed me to war with testimony at that time. He reminded me of the men of Ephraim:

> The men of Ephraim, though armed with bows, turned back on the day of battle; they did not keep God's covenant and refused to live by his law. **They forgot what he had done,** the wonders he had shown them.
>
> Psalm 78:9-11, emphasis added

They were prepared on the day of battle, but these men forgot the wonders God had done and the things He had shown them. In that difficult season of my life, I knew what I had to do. I would go to my bedroom, lay out all the bills before the Lord, and start reminding Him of His personal faithfulness to me all through the years. I listed every time I was in need and then recalled the miracle of how He came through for me. I reminded Him of every time my church leadership team had bills to pay, the staff salaries needed to be paid, etc., and how provision came in at the last minute. I remembered the testimonies of His faithfulness and spoke them back to Him. Then I declared to Him: *You are the same God yesterday, today, and forever.*

God responded and broke through for me then and He is also here for me today. I fight until I get a tangible breakthrough. I might not see the answer right away, but the heaviness lifts. When it does, I know that breakthrough is just around the corner.

I warred with testimony until I began to feel praise rise up within me. Once it did, I shouted and danced around *halal*-style—launching radical praise. That's a good habit for New Covenant happy prophets to establish. So I praised and praised and praised . . . and praised some more. A week later, a large unexpected check came in the mail. The Lord said, "That check came from the praise you began to release a week ago." It was sufficient to pay off all my bills, with enough left over to send me to a foreign country where I had wanted to go minister.

Boom, baby. That's the power of testimony.

During the eight months of waiting and pressing in as the financial debts were mounting, I was asked to take up the offering at a Sunday evening regional service. I certainly didn't feel like doing the offering that day because I didn't feel like the strong man of God. But I did it anyway . . . in faith. As I stood before the congregation, I publicly recounted all the testimonies of God's financial faithfulness in my life. It didn't *feel* like a great faith-building offering testimony. But the next day, I got word from my loan agent who announced that surprisingly, she had found a qualifying loan allowing me to get out of that strangling place of debt. God turned *everything* around after I faithfully declared the testimony. That's the power when we remember and recount how faithful He's been to us.

Know His Ways

Testimony doesn't change us if we don't recognize what it is trying to teach us. Declaring the testimony reveals the nature of God. Moses knew God's ways but the people of Israel only knew His acts.

> *He made known His ways to Moses, His acts*
> *to the children of Israel.*

> Psalms 103:7, NKJV

There is a difference. If we only know how to cry out because we desperately need rescuing, we risk being rebuked for our lack of faith. Jesus rescued the disciples crying out in the boat, but then rebuked them for their lack of faith. Why? He expected them to *know* His ways. He expected they would know that God Almighty was with them and that He had only good intentions and plans for them. He expected that they knew how much they were loved and that He wasn't going to allow anything that would harm them. He expected them to remember that the Messiah was in the boat *with* them, and that if God is *for* them, who could be against them? But, they didn't catch that.

I remember once I had just seen someone dramatically healed, but right after that, I was worrying and highly anxious about where the money for my bills was going to come from. At that moment God said to me, "Where did I just go, Keith? Did I leave the building? You just saw me perform a miracle and now you're worrying like I'm no longer with you."

Sometimes we, too, don't catch what the testimony is trying to teach us. If God was there for the healing, He'll be there to provide for the bills.

As prophets, we are to be the ones taking a heart posture of rest in times of trial because we know who God is. We know His ways. Remember Elisha when the enemy had surrounded the city and they were going to kill him?[26] He was just sitting there resting because he saw in the spirit all those who surrounded them. He could clearly see that there were more on his side defending him than the great numbers against him. He saw the heavenly chariots of fire and knew he had the ability to release them, if necessary. We are to be the ones who can rest as we trust God's ability to protect us.

We have to remember what He has done before, He intends to do again, because that is just the kind of God He is. He is our provider, our protector, and He is always for us. How can we be prophets who announce and release a new day and bring hope and joy if we aren't personally acquainted with His ways and walk in complete trust of our God? The power to remember His glorious testimonies of the past always unleashes the full provision we need into the present. God lavishly provided for us before, and He will certainly do it again. In just the same way we have warred with testimony, we will see His reward come again.

---

[26] See 2 Kings 6.

The Expectation of Rewards

Twenty

There is a passage where Elisha is rebuking his servant Gehazi for taking money and possessions when he wasn't supposed to.

> But Elisha said to him, "Was not my spirit with you when the man got down from his chariot to meet you? Is this the time to take money, or to accept clothes—or olive groves and vineyards, or flocks and herds, or male and female slaves?"
>
> 2 Kings 5:26

Life was not very good for Gehazi after this incident. He really paid for going after financial gain in such an ungodly way. As a result, he suffered the rest of his life with leprosy.

But I get something else very significant out of this story. If there is a time when you are *not* to receive gifts, then that means there must be a time when you *can*. Elisha knew the times to receive rewards. He must have experienced being blessed quite a few times. In the Prophet Samuel's day, when you went to see the seer, you always brought a gift. For some reason, we rarely see this kind of honor in our day. It seems we have no grid for prophets and gifts. If you do hear about a prophet who receives a gift or some kind of financial remuneration, people criticize how wrong it is.

But let's take a look at biblical rewards. The only time in Scripture a prophet *wasn't* to receive a gift was if he was taking it as a bribe to prophesy something he shouldn't. A prophet was instructed not to receive gifts in the form of a bribe so as to prevent him from wavering in delivering the full truth of God's message.

A Generous God

Let's consider prophets who did receive gifts: Daniel, Joseph, and Abraham, to name a few. God came to Abram (later changed to Abraham) and said:

> *Do not be afraid, Abram. I am your shield, your very great reward.*
>
> Genesis 15:1

He promised to personally be Abraham's "very great reward." It is God's nature to be exceedingly generous and to give gifts. He is very generous to His servants and prophets and we have many examples of His lavish provision for them in Scripture.

Because of this I am learning the joy of rewards where I actually expect gifts. That may seem a bit out of the ordinary, but how are you going to be a prophet if you can't expect a reward—even a "very great reward"? Some people express a false humility when they suggest that God's presence is enough for them. I agree one hundred percent that His presence is everything—more than enough! But sometimes, having the reward of a new vehicle after years of driving one that breaks down constantly is very much appreciated!

A Caring Father

God did that for me. He gave me a brand new car through a person I had just met. What a gift! A year or two before, another person had given me a Harley Davidson motorcycle that was almost brand new, and I also received a beautiful Steinway grand piano that I really love to play. Because these gifts were very costly, I have come to appreciate even more the generous nature of our God and have learned to accept them and receive them as His rewards.

I appreciate that God isn't solely concerned about our hearts being warmed by His presence. He actually cares about every concern and delight of our heart and the physical needs we have to live life. During the time that I received those three costly gifts, God was teaching me that I was His son and that He loves to give me gifts that bring me pleasure . . . not for any reason in particular, just because. Earlier in ministry, I had lost my motorcycle and had another car stolen, and I've spent many years in anxious concern about our very limited finances while actively engaged in Kingdom work. My wife and I are the kind of people who give generously because we love it! Being generous givers brings such a satisfaction of seeing others blessed. We have lived without financial abundance much of our married life. We have also lived with our household possessions packed away in long-term storage while we traveled to foreign nations to serve in ministry. We've joyfully given our time, talents, and lives for the advancement of His Kingdom while living with very little.

Expect a Return

What we've learned over the years is Dad loves to

reward those who serve Him. You can't be a person of faith without expecting to be rewarded. Hebrews 11:6 says:

> *And without faith it is impossible to please God, because anyone who comes to him must believe that he exists and that he rewards those who earnestly seek him.*

How can a prophet of God live a life that prophesies good things without an expectation to see good things in return? Where is the joy to stay in the fight? There has to be payoff. When we see the reward for what we have prayed for and fought for, we find such joy. I live for the reward. I know how to keep the testimonies alive, the thanksgiving, the praise, and the hope alive. But I live to see the reward.

Breakthrough Releases Breakthrough

Sometimes I get around a strong prophetic person who prophesies an amazing word to someone about a breakthrough in his or her finances. I may know the person they are prophesying over and know the word is a good word. It fits the person. But I also know the life of the person that is prophesying and I'm aware that they have not personally experienced a financial breakthrough. The difference between a word that carries an impartation on it and a word that gives a promise for a later date is the one delivering it. If the one delivering it has the proof of being rewarded in their own life and seeing God's faithfulness and then prophesies from that place, there is often a much greater breakthrough attached. Now God can certainly deliver a great word through someone who doesn't carry breakthrough, but the word a prophet delivers must also be true and activated in their own life. How can I give a word about someone else getting financial breakthrough when I personally haven't received it, experienced it, or don't expect that is how God rewards? It just doesn't match up.

The Joy of Rewards

I have discovered that some prophetic people have a poverty mindset. Where is the joy in that? Where is the reward? The joy is in the reward. There is joy in learning that Dad wants to bless your socks off. When you get your socks blessed off as a prophet, you are going to let everyone else in on the secret of how to get their socks blessed off. That is how it works. Prophets equip others. So their breakthrough becomes a corporate breakthrough. What a joy that is—to be the one who pioneers and perseveres through the hardship and misery of financial lack until you see the God of full provision and abundance come through. That has been my journey, and I carry a spirit of breakthrough in that area.

Like I said, I lived in financial lack for many years. Whoever said living in lack is living in faith? It isn't. There is a lot of anxiety when you must live that way. Living with barely enough is not a joyful lifestyle. That is not who God is. We know He is the God of more than enough. Sometimes we need to upgrade our view of God if we are going to see a breakthrough.

God told me years ago that He wanted to bless me, but I saw Him through the lens of a "poor" King. My examples of those serving God was in much lack and near poverty conditions, which translated my view of God's provision as "barely enough". This perspective of His provision for those who served Him was inhibiting His ability to bless me generously.

Discovering the God of Wealth

That sent me on a journey for a few years of discovering the God of wealth. Now I see that He is the God of abundant provision. Prophets are the ones who are supposed to see the provision of the Lord come through. We are the ones who receive the strategy to see the wealth unlocked from its storehouses. We prophesy it, we release it, because God shows us.

It was Elisha who could see the strategy to take earthen jars, pour oil that was readily available into the jars, and then sell those oil-filled jars at the market in order to see the debts of the widow paid off.[27] Elijah had to see that the supernatural miracle provision for the widow woman was in a loaf of bread. If she could just make him a loaf of bread first, Elijah instructed, then her flour and oil would not run out for a good long while.[28]

Prophets see the direct route to the abundant provision of wealth. We have to expect that God wants to reward His servants greatly and that He really cares about our daily physical needs. There is such joy when you receive a car, a motorcycle, a piano, a house, or whatever you need. It demonstrates the lovingkindness of a good Father to you personally. It lets you know that as a prophet, you are first a son or a daughter, and that as your Father in Heaven He wants you to know that He is caring for *all* your needs. In allowing Him to care for your needs, and letting Him love you in this way, you will find such authority to then release that revelation of His generous goodness and provision to others.

Don't hold back from allowing others to enjoy the

---

[27] See 2 Kings 4:1-7.
[28] See 1 Kings 17:7-16.

blessings of the Lord, either. Be willing to be blessed by learning how to receive gifts. See it as God's gift to you. Enjoy the reward of your labors. And then, pass it on.

He alone deserves all the glory—that is for certain— and our greatest joy is to thank Him for all His generous rewards and gifts as we cast our crowns before His feet. We are the privileged ones to give God *all* the glory. But why not do it from a place of His abundant blessings? Yes, I learned to be content with very little, but it sure is nice to know that it isn't the only season He has promised us. There is a season of generous abundance as well.

I want to make this announcement: This is *your* time for financial breakthrough. This is your moment where you have prayed the prayers, you have kept the faith, and now there is coming a reward—a great reward from your Father who cares for you. He is saying to you:

> Come in, good and faithful servant; enter
> into the joy of the Lord over you.

Learn to live in that place of His affirmation and love. Learn to live in His great pleasure over you. There is no greater joy than that.

Living in that place of His reward is key to moving forward. There are eternal pleasures at His right hand: joy in His presence forevermore. Have an expectation from today on of the Father delighting to give you good gifts . . . and anticipate the great joy in that.

The Joy of Being Human

Twenty-One

One of the challenges with the office of a prophet is moving into the joy of just being a regular person. But I believe there is a new day upon us where prophets are going to be able to enjoy just being normal people, able to let their guard down and enjoy others. It can be especially challenging in a church where people see you as "the prophet." But how can a prophet also just be a regular Joe within the congregation? Sometimes people come up to me asking for a prophetic word because they know they can get a good one. That puts a lot of pressure on me because I don't always want to be "on" as a prophet, but at the same time, I want to be generous with my gift. Most times I just want to be a part of the family of God and enjoy being known as a guy who has children, a lovely wife, and another life outside of the prophetic gift.

I have watched and heard other prophets who have shared their challenges of being in public ministry because people have a hard time letting that person just be and not continually pull on them for prophetic ministry. I remember early on one of my prophetess connections told me that I needed to not let people put on me the expectations to be the "prophet of fire" all the time. She said, "Don't let them expect you to be the one that always blows up a meeting. It may not happen that way every time, and it will steal your joy." This is part of the challenge of being a prophet when you truly have a gift from God.

Finding a Place to just "be"

Prophets want to be able to relate to others in a normal relationship apart from the prophetic gifting. Sometimes I want to be known as Keith the dad, Keith a great friend, Keith a great husband, Keith a fun guy, not just, Keith the prophet. We have to build into our culture a safe place for prophets to just *be*. There's a lot of joy in that as well.

I have a well-known prophet friend who does a lot of work at a prominent Christian television station. His challenge is being able to attend his church as the normal person he is apart from his public persona. Whenever he's at church or on the TV set, there are many people who come up to him for prophetic words. So if he wants to enjoy a church service he has to go to another church where nobody knows him. That is sad; it shouldn't be that way.

There has to be a place for prophets to feel at home and be normal. While it is important for a prophet to be valued and appreciated for their gift, sometimes the best way to value them is to treat them like a normal person. That really sets them at ease.

What the Prophet Really Needs

I remember being in a foreign country that really loved the prophetic gift. They would pay good money for a prophet to come to their country and they always provided first class accommodations in a really nice hotel, take them to great restaurants, buy them gifts, etc. They were very generous, but they had not learned how to truly honor the prophet. They would get upset at spending a lot of money on the prophet they invited only to learn he didn't enjoy the food at the place where they took him to eat. They would get upset if he didn't prophesy over *every* single person on cue. They would get upset if he asked for an adjustment in the pre-arranged meetings with its impossible and exhausting preaching schedule.

I felt like I needed to coach these pastors and leaders by exhorting them: "If you truly want to honor the prophet you've invited and get the reward for honoring him, then find out what his specific needs are as he is a guest in your nation. For instance, find out what type of meals he needs to perform at his best. He may have trouble with specific foods, so ask him. If he isn't willing to prophesy over every single person, there may be a reason you're not aware of. So honor that. Try to create an environment that honors the prophet and his gift. By doing that, you are honoring God, and you will receive all you were hoping for from your guest and so much more."

I tried my best to get them to see that I was not a robotic prophetic machine, encouraging them instead to just come hang out with me for a simple meal. I love sharing a meal together with friends and talking about people's families, their life, home, etc. I want them to know about mine as well. That's a normal part of being relational, and those are the opportunities that bring the best out of me. It's environments like these that often activates my prophetic gift without even trying. When I am in a place where people truly care about me as a person, and there's a relaxed exchange of conversation, then I am able to function so much better. Prophecy often flows so easily at the dinner table than in a public meeting place where you are expected to prophesy over every person because it is your "job" and you feel obligated.

The Human Side of the Prophet

We must create atmospheres that honor prophets as normal human beings instead of seeing them only functioning in their supernatural gift. In order for that to happen though, we, as prophets, must be vulnerable by allowing others to see us in our humanity aside from our gifts by letting them into our world. We must find ways to enjoy each other as friends and family.

Another one of my prophetic friends has so much wisdom that I have gleaned from for so many years. It is really hard for me not to want to ask him questions every time I am with him. I want to get answers for the things I am trying to figure out. When I'm with him, it sometimes feels like I'm talking to God—getting Heaven's wisdom and direction. I have had to realize I can't do that all the time, though. I had to renegotiate the relationship because I wanted something different out of it. We both have had to rewire our thinking in the relationship in order to relate as friends and actually learn to enjoy each other as friends aside from our prophetic gift. It doesn't mean I can't receive the wisdom he carries. I do. It just means that it doesn't take up the majority of our time together nor does it totally define who we are.

None of us like to be the one-trick pony. The problem is if you're not doing your one trick, then you don't know how to function in relationship outside of that. It means the relationship is going to be functionally driven. But sustainable joy only comes as you are able to be who you are as a normal person, where you can be relaxed in your community environment without pressure to perform.

The Joy of Being You

I'm praying for you, that you will understand who you really are apart from your prophetic gift, that you will enjoy the person you are, enjoy who others are, find the right ones to hang with, and stay in the journey of being a happy prophet. It may be a fight, but it is well worth it, because it is a good fight, a joyful fight, and a fight you are destined to win.

You are so needed in this day and time. How vital it is that you reset the framework of how you see the prophetic and how the prophetic gift and ministry is viewed. My prayer and purpose for writing this book is that you will be able to see the prophetic through the lens of joy.

I pray that you know the fullness of joy in His glorious presence, and may His delight in you increase your joy more and more to ever be His happy prophet.

About the Author

Keith Ferrante is a prophetic voice who travels internationally speaking in churches, conferences, ministry schools, and other venues. He carries a message of freedom for the Body of Christ helping to bring revival and reformation. He is a prophetic voice that carries a breaker anointing to open up the heavens and brings timely corporate and personal prophetic words. Keith has developed many resources that offer a fresh perspective on the prophetic, supernatural Kingdom-character, and spiritual gifting. Keith is passionate to see the fullness of Heaven's atmosphere here on earth and brings people into divine reality through joyful glory encounters, impartation, and signs and wonders.

Keith is the founder and director of Emerging Prophets, a ministry that provides resources for highly gifted prophetic individuals. The ministry helps them discover whether or not they are a prophet, what kind of a prophet they are, and provides resources and lessons that help develop the much-needed character to move from the calling of prophet to the office of prophet.

Keith is also a prophetic life consultant, assisting highly motivated individuals and influencers to achieve breakthrough in their personal and spiritual life, business, and position of influence.

Emerging Prophet School

If you are interested in developing your prophetic call or discovering if you are a prophet, visit our website to find out how you can sign up for a module on our online school or attend a regional Emerging Prophet school near you. If you are interested in personally being developed as an emerging prophet, we also offer coaching for developing prophets, as well as marketplace leaders. If you are interested in hosting an Emerging Prophet weekend intensive to introduce the concept of developing prophets in your area, please contact us. Also if you are interested in starting an Emerging Prophet School in your area, we would love to chat with you.

If you would like to host Keith Ferrante or one of the Emerging Prophet trainers to minister in your area, please contact us at:

www.emergingprophets.com

More Resources from Keith Ferrante

Books

- *Embracing the Emerging Prophets*
- *There Must Be More*
- *Keys to Abundance*
- *Restoring the Father's Heart*
- *Reforming the Church From a House to a Home*
- *Emerging Prophets: Discovering Your Identity Workbook*
- *Emerging Prophets: Discovering Your Metron Workbook*
- *Emerging Prophets: Calling to Office Discovery Workbook*

Music CDs

- "Unveiled Mysteries"
- "Where You Are"
- "New Sounds"
- "Falling into You"
- "Songs From Heaven"

Available at our website:

www.emergingprophets.com

Made in the USA
Columbia, SC
15 September 2019